# Indiana

# interactive
## SCIENCE

When threatened,
swallowtail caterpillars
can release a bad smell
to keep away enemies!

PEARSON

Glenview, Illinois  •  Boston, Massachusetts  •  Chandler, Arizona  •  Upper Saddle River, New Jersey

# Authors

## You are an author!

You are one of the authors of this book. You can write in this book! You can take notes in this book! You can draw in it too! This book will be yours to keep.

Fill in the information below to tell about yourself. Then write your autobiography. An autobiography tells about you and the kinds of things you like to do.

**My Photo**

**Name** .................................................................................

**School** ................................................................................

**Town, State** .........................................................................

**Autobiography** .....................................................................

..................................................................................................

..................................................................................................

..................................................................................................

..................................................................................................

..................................................................................................

..................................................................................................

Credits appear on pages EM17–EM18, which constitute an extension of this copyright page.

**ON THE COVER:**
When threatened, swallowtail caterpillars can release a bad smell to keep away enemies!

ISBN-13: 978-0-328-52093-0
ISBN-10: 0-328-52093-4
6 7 8 9 10 V011 19 18 17 16 15 14

## Program Authors

**DON BUCKLEY, M.Sc.**
*Information and Communications Technology Director,*
*The School at Columbia University, New York, New York*
Mr. Buckley has been at the forefront of K–12 educational technology for nearly two decades. A founder of New York City Independent School Technologists (NYCIST) and long-time chair of New York Association of Independent Schools' annual IT conference, he has taught students on two continents and created multimedia and Internet-based instructional systems for schools worldwide.

**ZIPPORAH MILLER, M.A.Ed.**
*Associate Executive Director for Professional Programs and Conferences, National Science Teachers Association, Arlington, Virginia*
Associate executive director for professional programs and conferences at NSTA, Ms. Zipporah Miller is a former K–12 science supervisor and STEM coordinator for the Prince George's County Public School District in Maryland. She is a science education consultant who has overseen curriculum development and staff training for more than 150 district science coordinators.

**MICHAEL J. PADILLA, Ph.D.**
*Associate Dean and Director, Eugene P. Moore School of Education, Clemson University, Clemson, South Carolina*
A former middle school teacher and a leader in middle school science education, Dr. Michael Padilla has served as president of the National Science Teachers Association and as a writer of the National Science Education Standards. He is professor of science education at Clemson University. As lead author of the *Science Explorer* series, Dr. Padilla has inspired the team in developing a program that promotes student inquiry and meets the needs of today's students.

**KATHRYN THORNTON, Ph.D.**
*Professor and Associate Dean, School of Engineering and Applied Science, University of Virginia, Charlottesville, Virginia*
Selected by NASA in May 1984, Dr. Kathryn Thornton is a veteran of four space flights. She has logged more than 975 hours in space, including more than 21 hours of extravehicular activity. As an author on the *Scott Foresman Science* series, Dr. Thornton's enthusiasm for science has inspired teachers around the globe.

**MICHAEL E. WYSESSION, Ph.D.**
*Associate Professor of Earth and Planetary Science, Washington University, St. Louis, Missouri*
An author on more than 50 scientific publications, Dr. Wysession was awarded the prestigious Packard Foundation Fellowship and Presidential Faculty Fellowship for his research in geophysics. Dr. Wysession is an expert on Earth's inner structure and has mapped various regions of Earth using seismic tomography. He is known internationally for his work in geoscience education and outreach.

## Instructional Design Author

**GRANT WIGGINS, Ed.D.**
*President, Authentic Education, Hopewell, New Jersey*
Dr. Wiggins is a co-author with Jay McTighe of *Understanding by Design, 2nd Edition* (ASCD 2005). His approach to instructional design provides teachers with a disciplined way of thinking about curriculum design, assessment, and instruction that moves teaching from covering content to ensuring understanding.
UNDERSTANDING BY DESIGN® and UbD™ are trademarks of ASCD, and are used under license.

## Planet Diary Author

**JACK HANKIN**
*Science/Mathematics Teacher, The Hilldale School, Daly City, California*
*Founder, Planet Diary Web site*
Mr. Hankin is the creator and writer of Planet Diary, a science current events Web site. Mr. Hankin is passionate about bringing science news and environmental awareness into classrooms.

## Activities Author

**KAREN L. OSTLUND, Ph.D.**
*Advisory Council, Texas Natural Science Center, College of Natural Sciences, The University of Texas at Austin*
Dr. Ostlund has more than 35 years of experience teaching at elementary, middle school, and university levels. Previously she was Director of WINGS Online (Welcoming Interns and Novices with Guidance and Support) and Director of the UTeach | Dell Center for New Teacher Success at the University of Texas at Austin. She was Director of the Center for Science Education at the University of Texas at Arlington, President of the Council of Elementary Science International, and member, Board of Directors, National Science Teachers Association. As an author of *Scott Foresman Science*, Dr. Ostlund was instrumental in developing inquiry activities.

## ELL Consultant

**JIM CUMMINS, Ph.D.**
*Professor and Canada Research Chair, Curriculum, Teaching and Learning Department at the University of Toronto*
Dr. Cummins focuses on literacy development in multilingual schools and the role of technology in learning. *Interactive Science* incorporates research-based principles for integrating language with the teaching of academic content based on his work.

# Reviewers

## Program Consultants

**WILLIAM BROZO, Ph.D.**
*Professor of Literacy, Graduate School of Education, George Mason University, Fairfax, Virginia.*
Dr. Brozo is the author of numerous articles and books on literacy development. He co-authors a column in The Reading Teacher and serves on the editorial review board of the Journal of Adolescent & Adult Literacy.

**KRISTI ZENCHAK, M.S.**
*Biology Instructor, Oakton Community College, Des Plaines, Illinois*
Kristi Zenchak helps elementary teachers incorporate science, technology, engineering, and math activities into the classroom. STEM activities that produce viable solutions to real-world problems not only motivate students but also prepare students for future STEM careers. Ms. Zenchak helps elementary teachers understand the basic science concepts, and provides STEM activities that are easy to implement in the classroom.

## Content Reviewers

**Paul Beale, Ph.D.**
Department of Physics
University of Colorado
Boulder, Colorado

**Joy Branlund, Ph.D.**
Department of Earth Science
Southwestern Illinois College
Granite City, Illinois

**Constance Brown, Ph.D**
Atmospheric Science Program
Geography Department
Indiana University
Bloomington, Indiana

**Dana Dudle, Ph.D.**
Biology Department
DePauw University
Greencastle, Indiana

**Rick Duhrkopf, Ph. D.**
Department of Biology
Baylor University
Waco, Texas

**Mark Henriksen, Ph.D.**
Physics Department
University of Maryland
Baltimore, Maryland

**Andrew Hirsch, Ph.D.**
Department of Physics
Purdue University
W. Lafayette, Indiana

**Linda L. Cronin Jones, Ph.D.**
School of Teaching & Learning
University of Florida
Gainesville, Florida

**T. Griffith Jones, Ph.D.**
College of Education
University of Florida
Gainesville, Florida

**Candace Lutzow-Felling, Ph.D.**
Director of Education
State Arboretum of Virginia &
   Blandy Experimental Farm
Boyce, VA

**Cortney V. Martin, Ph.D.**
Virginia Polytechnic Institute
Blacksburg, Virginia

**Sadredin Moosavi, Ph.D.**
University of Massachusetts
   Dartmouth
Fairhaven, Massachusetts

**Klaus Newmann, Ph.D.**
Department of Geological
   Sciences
Ball State University
Muncie, Indiana

**Scott M. Rochette, Ph.D.**
Department of the Earth
   Sciences
SUNY College at Brockport
Brockport, New York

**Karyn Rogers, Ph.D.**
Department of Geological
   Sciences
University of Missouri
Columbia, Missouri

**Laurence Rosenhein, Ph.D.**
Dept. of Chemistry and Physics
Indiana State University
Terre Haute, Indiana

**Sara Seager, Ph.D.**
Department of Planetary Science
   and Physics
Massachusetts Institute of
   Technology
Cambridge, MA

**William H. Steinecker, Ph.D.**
Research Scholar
Miami University
Oxford, Ohio

**Paul R. Stoddard, Ph.D.**
Department of Geology and
   Environmental Geosciences
Northern Illinois University
DeKalb, Illinois

**Laurence Rosenhein, Ph. D.**
Department of Chemistry
Indiana State University
Terre Haute, Indiana

**Janet Vaglia, Ph. D.**
Department of Biology
DePauw University
Greencastle, Indiana

**Ed Zalisko, Ph.D.**
Professor of Biology
Blackburn College
Carlinville, Illinois

# Built especially for
# Indiana

Indiana *Interactive Science* covers 100% of Indiana's Academic Standards for Science without extraneous content. Built on feedback from Indiana educators, *Interactive Science* focuses on what is important to Indiana teachers and students, creating a personal, relevant, and engaging classroom experience.

## Indiana K-8 Science Teacher Advisory Board

**Jodi Allen**
Glen Acres Elementary School
Lafayette, IN

**Rick Dubbs**
Monrovia Middle School
Monrovia, IN

**Margaret Flack**
Vincennes University
    Jasper Campus
Jasper, IN

**Michael Gibson**
New Haven Middle School
New Haven, IN

**Jill Hatcher**
Spring Mill Elementary School
Indianapolis, IN

**Jamie Hooten**
Lincoln Elementary School
Bedford, IN

**Jamil Odom**
Mary Bryan Elementary School
Indianapolis, IN

**Mike Robards**
Franklin Community Middle School
Franklin, IN

**Richard Towle**
Noblesville Middle School
Noblesville, IN

## K-8 National Master Teacher Board

**Tricia Burke**
E. F. Young Elementary School
Chicago, IL

**Lisa Catandella**
Brentwood UFSD
Brentwood, NY

**Karen Clements**
Lynch Elementary School
Winchester, MA

**Emily Compton**
Park Forest Middle School
Baton Rouge, LA

**Pansy Cowder**
Lincoln Magnet School
Plant City, FL

**Georgi Delgadillo**
East Valley School District
Spokane, WA

**Dr. Richard Fairman**
McGregor School of Education
Antioch University Midwest
Yellow Springs, OH

**Joe Fescatore**
Green Elementary School
La Mesa, CA

**Mimi Halferty**
Gorzycki Middle School
Austin, TX

**Christy Herring**
Prairie Trace Elementary School
Carmel, IN

**Treva Jeffries**
Toledo Public Schools
Toledo, OH

**James Kuhl**
Central Square Middle School
Central Square, NY

**Dr. Patsy Latin**
Caddo Public School District
Shreveport, LA

**Greg Londot**
Hidden Hills Elementary School
Phoenix, AZ

**Stan Melby**
Sheridan Road Elementary
Fort Sill, OK

**Bonnie Mizell**
Howard Middle School
Orlando, FL

**Dr. Joel Palmer**
Mesquite ISD
Mesquite, TX

**Leslie Pohley**
Largo Middle School
Largo, FL

**Susan Pritchard**
Washington Middle School
La Habra, CA

**Anne Rice**
Woodland Middle School
Gurnee, IL

**Adrienne Sawyer**
Chesapeake Public Schools
Chesapeake, VA

**Richard Towle**
Noblesville Middle School
Noblesville, IN

**Dr. Madhu Uppal**
Schaumburg School District
Schaumburg, IL

**Maria Valdez**
Mark Twain Elementary School
Wheeling, IL

**Viv Wayne**
Montgomery County Public Schools
Rockville, MD

# Indiana Unit A
## Science, Engineering, and Technology

# The Nature of Science

*Scientists can dive to study ocean life.*

**①** myscienceonline.com

🐢 UntamedScience™
Watch the Ecogeeks as
they learn about the nature
of science.

**Got it?** ⏱ 60-Second Video
Watch and learn about the
nature of science.

**Envision It!**
See what you already know
about the nature of science.

**Memory Match**
Mix-and-match vocabulary
practice

**I Will Know...**
See how the key concepts of
the nature of science come
to life.

# Technology and Design

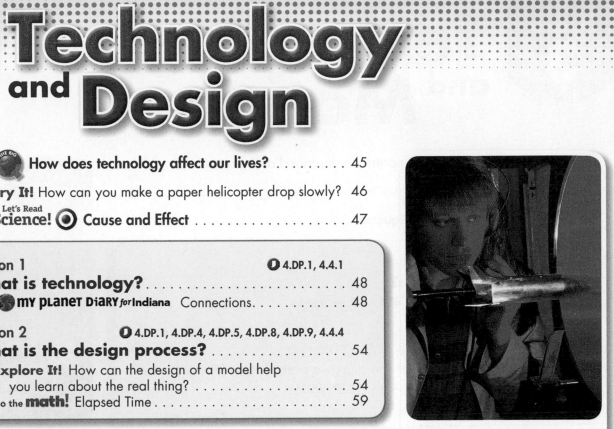

*Engineers test prototypes when designing products.*

❶ mYscienceonLine.com

🐸 UntamedScience™
Ecogeeks answer your
questions about technology
and design.

Got *it?* ⏱ 60-Second Video
Review lessons about
technology and design
in 60 seconds!

▸Explore It! Animation
Quick and easy online
experiments about
technology and design

▸Investigate It! Virtual Lab
Investigate how materials
affect a boat's design and
function.

🌍 mY PLaneT DiaRY
Find out more about
technologies that improve
car safety.

# Technology and Motion

*Amusement parks have rides that move in different ways.*

🟠 **myscienceonline.com**

**UntamedScience™**
Watch the Ecogeeks learn about technology and motion.

**Got it?** ⏱ **60-Second Video**
Lessons about technology and motion reviewed in a minute!

**Envision It!**
See what you already know about technology and motion.

**Explore It!** Animation
Quick and easy online experiments about technology and motion

**Vocabulary Smart Cards**
Mix-and-match technology and motion vocabulary

Indiana

Chapter 4

Indiana Unit B
Physical Science

Indiana Unit B Physical Science . . . . . . . . . . 115
Apply It! How is motion affected by mass? . . . . . 156
Indiana Unit B Performance-Based Assessment 160

# Energy, Heat, and Electricity

Light bulbs transform electrical energy into forms we can use.

**myscienceonline.com**

**Untamed Science™**
Watch the Ecogeeks as they learn about energy, heat, and electricity.

**Got it? 60-Second Video**
One-minute videos summarizing energy, heat, and electricity topics

**Envision It!**
Find out what you already know about energy, heat, and electricity.

**I Will Know...**
See what you've learned about energy, heat, and electricity.

**Explore It! Animation**
Explore energy, heat, and electricity in a new way!

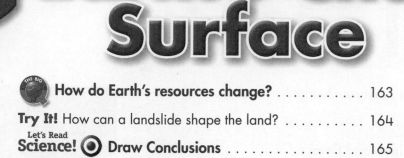

# Earth's Changing Surface

*The mineral halite is commonly known as rock salt.*

❶ **mYscienceonLine.com**

**UntamedScience**
Watch the Ecogeeks as they learn about Earth's changing surface.

**Got it?** ⏱ **60-Second Video**
One-minute videos about Earth's changing surface

**Envision It!**
Find out what you already know about Earth's changing surface.

**Explore It! Animation**
Explore Earth's changing surface in a new way!

**I Will Know...**
See what you've learned about Earth's changing surface.

**Indiana Unit D**
Life Science

# Interactions

*Purple loosestrife crowds
out native plants in parts
of Indiana.*

**❶ myscienceonline.com**

**UntamedScience™**
Go on a science adventure
with the Ecogeeks!

**Got it?** 🕐 **60-Second Video**
Review each lesson in 60
seconds!

**Envision It!**
See what you already know
about science.

**Explore It!** **Animation**
Quick and easy online
experiments

**I Will Know...**
See how key concepts of each
lesson are brought to life!

# "This is your book. You can write in it!"

# interactive
## SCIENCE

## Big Question

At the start of each chapter you will see two questions—an **Engaging Question** and a **Big Question.** Just like a scientist, you will predict an answer to the Engaging Question. Each Big Question will help you start thinking about Indiana's Big Ideas of science. Look for the symbol throughout the chapter!

### What affects motion?

**Indiana**

**Chapter 3**

## Technology and Motion

**Try It!** How can you measure motion?

**Lesson 1** What is motion?

**Lesson 2** What is speed?
4.4.2

**Lesson 3** How do forces affect motion?
4.4.1, 4.4.3

**Investigate It!** How can friction affect motion?

These cyclists are riding on a circular racing track. This track has curves and banks so that the cyclists can move very quickly.

**Predict** What might affect the cyclists' motion?

_____

_____

How can motion be described and measured?

myscienceonline.com

## Let's Read Science!

You will see a page like this toward the beginning of each chapter. It will show you how to use a reading skill that will help you understand what you read.

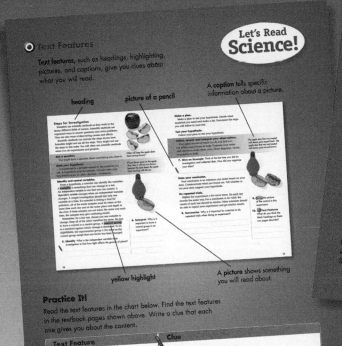

## Vocabulary Smart Cards

Go to the end of the chapter and cut out your own set of **Vocabulary Smart Cards.** Write a sentence, draw a picture, or use a vocabulary strategy to learn the word. Play a game with a classmate to practice using the word!

myscienceonline.com | Untamed Science™

Look for **MyScienceOnline.com** technology options.
At MyScienceOnline.com you can immerse yourself in virtual environments, get extra practice, and even blog about current events in science.

# "Engage with the page!"

## interactive SCIENCE

### Envision It!

At the beginning of each lesson, at the top of the page, you will see an **Envision It!** interactivity that gives you the opportunity to circle, draw, write, or respond to the Envision It! question.

---

Lesson 4

## How do organisms get and use energy?

3.3.1 Observe and classify common Indiana organisms as producers, consumers, decomposers, predator and prey based on their relationships and interactions with other organisms in their ecosystem. 3140 3.NS.9

### Envision It!

I will know how plants use energy from the sun.

**Words to Know**
photosynthesis
cellular respiration

Tell how you think plants get the energy they need to live.

---

### my PLANET DiARY for Indiana

## DISCOVERY

What comes to mind when you think of corn? You might think of corn on the cob, popcorn, or cornbread. However, corn is not just food. Scientists have discovered that it can also be used to produce a liquid fuel called ethanol. Ethanol is a type of biofuel. Biofuels are fuels made from living things. Other plants used to make biofuel are soy and sugarcane. Biofuels are more environmentally friendly than other fuels, such as gasoline. Because gasoline-powered vehicles produce air pollution, using biofuels instead might help preserve Earth's environment.

How do you think biofuels might affect your life?

myscienceonline.com | my PLANET DiARY    254

### Energy Sources

What is your favorite type of green salad? You might like one made of spinach. Perhaps you choose iceberg lettuce or crispy romaine lettuce. Spinach, iceberg lettuce, and romaine lettuce are all types of leaves. A leaf is a major plant part. Unlike animals, plants make their own food. Most of the food that a plant makes is made in the plant's leaves.

When you eat spinach or lettuce leaves, your body gets their energy. Your body cells need this energy to carry out its many functions. The energy you get is stored in the leaves. Where did the leaves get this energy? It came from the sun in the form of sunlight. The sun is Earth's primary energy source. The plant used the sunlight's energy to make its food, which it uses to grow. This form of energy passes on to you when you eat the leaves.

**1. Identify** Where does the stored energy in these cabbage leaves come from?

**2. Explain** How does a plant get its food?

cabbage

myscienceonline.com | Envision It!    255

---

## my PLANET DiARY

**My Planet Diary** interactivities will introduce you to amazing scientists, fun facts, and important discoveries in science. They will also help you to overcome common misconceptions about science concepts.

## Read See DO!

After reading small chunks of information, stop to check your understanding. The visuals help teach about what you read. Answer questions, underline text, draw pictures, or label models.

### Volcanoes

Sometimes molten rock, or lava, comes out of Earth's surface. A **volcano** is an opening in Earth's crust where gases, ash, and molten rock can reach the surface. A volcano can take many years to form. However, a volcanic eruption can change Earth's surface quickly. Most volcanoes form underwater where two plates pull apart. However, volcanoes on land often form at areas where two plates meet and one slides underneath the other.

### How volcanoes form

Earth's mantle is almost entirely solid. But when one plate moves below another plate, it brings down water that helps the rock partially melt. The rock becomes a hot liquid material called magma. Magma is lighter than solid rock, so it quickly rises upward. When a volcano erupts, the magma reaches the surface and is called lava.

**4. Identify** Find and label another possible vent on this volcano.

**5. ⊙ Draw Conclusions** Select three facts from the text above. Then draw a conclusion.

| Facts | Conclusion |
| --- | --- |
|  |  |
|  |  |
|  |  |

### Effects of volcanoes

Volcanoes can form on continents. They can also build from the ocean floor. A volcanic island forms when a volcano reaches the surface of the water. The state of Hawaii is a string of islands formed in this way.

Volcanoes can do more than ooze fountains of lava. Gases, such as water vapor and carbon dioxide, are often mixed with the lava. Trapped gases can have enough pressure to blow apart the side of a volcano during an eruption. These trapped gases can push lava high into the air. While it is still in the air, this lava may cool into ash or rocks. However, not all volcanic eruptions are violent.

Volcanic eruptions can also affect the climate. In 1991, Mount Pinatubo in the Philippines erupted. It sent huge amounts of ash and other particles into the atmosphere. These particles reduced the amount of sunlight that reached Earth. As a result, average temperatures were cooler around the world by as much as one degree for more than a year.

**6. ⊙ Cause and Effect** Draw an example of how Mount Pinatubo's eruption might have reduced temperatures.

*Layers of cooled rock from eruptions can form a cone shape around a volcano.*

*A spot from which lava erupts is called a vent.*

*A bowl-shaped area, or crater, may form around the main vent.*

184 myscienceonline.com | I Will Know...

185

---

### Velocity and Acceleration

Some objects change speed *and direction*. **Velocity** is both the speed and the direction an object is moving. Some words that describe direction are *north, south, east,* and *west*. Others are *left, right, up,* and *down*.

Any change in the speed or direction of an object's motion is acceleration. Starting, speeding up, and slowing down are accelerations. The roller coaster accelerates as it speeds up or slows down. It is changing speed. A roller coaster on a curved path accelerates even if its speed does not change. That is because it changes direction as it moves around the curve.

**7. Decide** Which of the following is NOT an example of an acceleration?
  a. An airplane moving at the same speed in the same direction
  b. An airplane slowing its speed and moving down to land
  c. An airplane slowing its speed and moving in the same direction

**8. Summarize** What are two things that must be measured in order to find an object's velocity?

**9. Illustrate** Look at the roller coaster on the opposite page. Draw a solid arrow where the roller coaster slows down, and a dotted arrow where the coaster speeds up.

**10. ⊙ Sequence** First, the roller coaster slows as it moves up to the top of the loop. Write what happens next.

#### Do the math!

**Calculate Percentages**

Race cars travel quickly around racetracks. To determine how much of the track has been traveled, fill in the chart by finding the fraction, decimal, and percentage. The first row is done for you.

| Amount of Track Traveled | | |
| --- | --- | --- |
| Fraction | Decimal | Percentage |
| 80/100 | 0.80 | 80% |
| 50/100 | 0.50 | |
| 35/100 | | |
| | 0.25 | 25% |

**Got it?**

**11. Produce** How do you calculate average speed?

**12. Distinguish** What is the difference between speed and velocity?

● **Stop!** I need help with

❚❚ **Wait!** I have a question about

► **Go!** Now I know

86 myscienceonline.com | Got it? | 60-Second Video

myscienceonline.com | Got it? Quiz 87

## Do the math!

Scientists commonly use math as a tool to help them answer science questions. You can practice skills that you are learning in math class right in your Interactive Science Student Edition!

## Got it?

At the end of each lesson you will have a chance to evaluate your own progress! After answering the **Got it?** questions, think about how you are doing. At this point you can stop, wait, or go on to the next lesson.

# "Have fun! Be a scientist!"

## interactive SCIENCE

### Try It!

At the start of every chapter, you will have the chance to do a hands-on inquiry lab. The lab will provide you with experiences that will prepare you for the chapter lessons or may raise a new question in your mind.

### Explore It!

Before you start reading the lesson, **Explore It!** activities provide you with an opportunity to first explore the content!

# Design It!

The **Design It!** activity has you use the engineering design process to find solutions to problems. By identifying the problem, doing research, and developing possible solutions, you will design, construct, and test a prototype for a real world problem. Communicate your evidence through graphs, tables, drawings, and prototypes and identify ways to make your solution better.

STEM activities are found throughout core and ancillary materials.

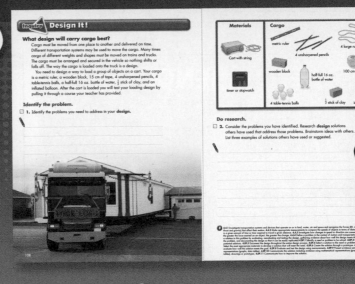

# Investigate It!

At the end of every chapter, a Directed Inquiry lab gives you a chance to put together everything you've learned in the chapter. Using the activity card, apply design principles in the Guided version to Modify Your Investigation or the Open version to Develop Your Own Investigation. Whether you need a lot of support from your teacher or you're ready to explore on your own, there are fun hands-on activities that match your interests.

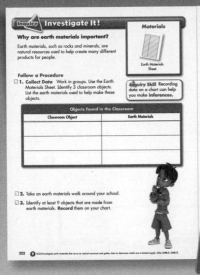

# Apply It!

At the end of every unit, an Open Inquiry lab gives you a chance to explore science using scientific methods.

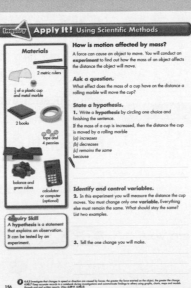

# "Go online anytime!"

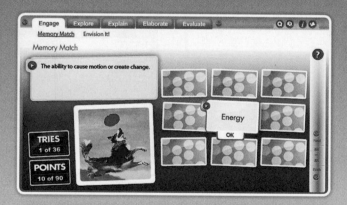

## Here's how you log in...

**1** Go to www.myscienceonline.com.

**2** Log in with your username and password.

Username: _____

Password: _____

**3** Click on your program and select your chapter.

## Check it out!

### Watch a Video!

**UntamedScience™** Join the Ecogeeks on their video adventure.

**Got it?** 60-Second Video Review each lesson in 60 seconds.

### Go Digital for Inquiry!

**Explore It!** Simulation Watch the lab online.

**Investigate It!** Virtual Lab Do the lab online.

### Show What You Know!

**Got it?** Quiz Take a quick quiz and get instant feedback.

**ISTEP+ Practice** Prepare for the "big test."

**Writing for Science** Write to help you unlock the Big Question.

### Get Excited About Science!

**The Big Question** Share what you think about the Big Question.

**my planet diary** Connect to the world of science.

**Envision It!** Connect to what you already know before you start each lesson.

**Memory Match** Play a game to build your vocabulary.

### Get Help!

**my science**  **coach** Get help at your level.

# Science, Engineering, and Technology

# Where is the scientist?

# The Nature of Science

Indiana

Chapter 1

**Try It!** How do scientists make observations?

**Lesson 1** What questions do scientists ask?
4.NS.1, 4.NS.4, 4.NS.6

**Lesson 2** How do scientists use tools?
4.NS.4, 4.NS.5

**Lesson 3** How do scientists answer questions?
4.NS.2, 4.NS.6, 4.NS.9

**Lesson 4** How do scientists draw conclusions?
4.NS.7, 4.NS.8, 4.NS.9

**Investigate It!** What affects how many times a pendulum swings?

Scientists observe the natural world. Through observation they can learn about things such as what kinds of plants and animals live in an area. They can also learn how those plants and animals interact.

**Predict** What do you think these student scientists might ask about this environment? Why?

........................................................................

........................................................................

........................................................................

**What is science?**

myscienceonline.com | Untamed Science

3

## How do scientists make observations?

☑ **1. Observe** a stapler or another object your teacher selects.

☑ **2.** Write 10 true statements about the object.

1. ......................................................................
2. ......................................................................
3. ......................................................................
4. ......................................................................
5. ......................................................................
6. ......................................................................
7. ......................................................................
8. ......................................................................
9. ......................................................................
10. ......................................................................

**Inquiry Skill**
Based on your careful
**observations** you can
make true statements.

☑ **3.** Work in a group. Put an ✗ by the true statements
that were written by more than one person.

## Explain Your Results

**4.** UNLOCK THE BIG How did working in a group
help you make better **observations**?

......................................................................

......................................................................

......................................................................

......................................................................

......................................................................

**4.NS.3** Plan and carry out investigations as a class, in small groups or independently, often over a period of several class lessons.

Text features, such as headings, labels, pictures, and captions, give you clues about what you will read.

Let's Read
## Science!

A **heading** tells what the content that follows is about.

A **picture** shows something you will read about.

A **caption** tells specific information about a picture.

Lightning Lab

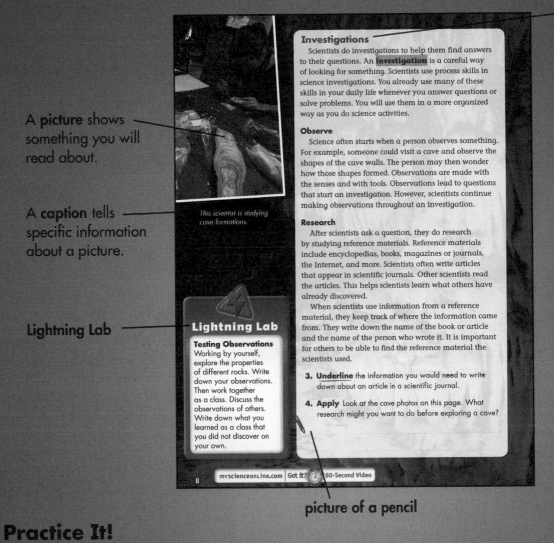

### Investigations

Scientists do investigations to help them find answers to their questions. An **investigation** is a careful way of looking for something. Scientists use process skills in science investigations. You already use many of these skills in your daily life whenever you answer questions or solve problems. You will use them in a more organized way as you do science activities.

### Observe

Science often starts when a person observes something. For example, someone could visit a cave and observe the shapes of the cave walls. The person may then wonder how those shapes formed. Observations are made with the senses and with tools. Observations lead to questions that start an investigation. However, scientists continue making observations throughout an investigation.

### Research

After scientists ask a question, they do research by studying reference materials. Reference materials include encyclopedias, books, magazines or journals, the Internet, and more. Scientists often write articles that appear in scientific journals. Other scientists read the articles. This helps scientists learn what others have already discovered.

When scientists use information from a reference material, they keep track of where the information came from. They write down the name of the book or article and the name of the person who wrote it. It is important for others to be able to find the reference material the scientists used.

3. **Underline** the information you would need to write down about an article in a scientific journal.

4. **Apply** Look at the cave photos on this page. What research might you want to do before exploring a cave?

*This scientist is studying cave formations.*

### ⚠ Lightning Lab

**Testing Observations**
Working by yourself, explore the properties of different rocks. Write down your observations. Then work together as a class. Discuss the observations of others. Write down what you learned as a class that you did not discover on your own.

8 | myscienceonline.com | Got It? | 60-Second Video

picture of a pencil

## Practice It!

Find the text features in the textbook page shown above.
Write a clue that each one gives you about the content.

| Feature | Clue |
|---|---|
| caption | tells me that a scientist is shown in the picture |
| picture of a pencil | |
| Lightning Lab | |

# What questions do scientists ask?

**4.NS.1** Make predictions and formulate testable questions. **4.NS.4** Perform investigations using appropriate tools and technology that will extend the senses. **4.NS.6** Test predictions with multiple trials.

## Envision It!

**Tell** what questions scientists might ask about this rock structure.

## my planeT DiaRY

The Paiute name for it is Paxa Uipi. You know it as the Grand Canyon. The Grand Canyon is located in the state of Arizona.

It is 446 kilometers long and ranges in width from 180 meters to nearly 29 kilometers. It is, on average, 1.6 kilometers deep. The canyon walls reveal layer after colorful layer of rock, nearly 40 of them. The oldest rock, at the bottom of the canyon, is the Vishnu schist. It is approximately 1.7 billion years old.

The Grand Canyon is clearly a wonder of the natural world. People from all over the world come to see this beautiful place.

Examine the statistics listed above. What questions might they make you want to ask about the Grand Canyon?

........................................................................

........................................................................

myscienceonLine.com | my planeT DiaRY

I will know what questions scientists ask. I will know how scientists find answers to their questions.

## Words to Know

inquiry
investigation

## Questions

Science includes **inquiry,** or the process of asking questions and searching for answers. Scientists ask questions about what they observe in the natural world. Someone looks at something carefully and asks about it. For example, a scientist studying Earth might think of a number of questions to ask. *How do islands form? What kinds of rock are on Earth's surface?*

Scientists first study what other scientists have already learned about the answers to their questions. Then scientists do experiments and make observations to find answers. They keep records of their observations and experiments. Keeping records can help them share what they learn with others.

**2. Ask Questions** What question do you think these scientists might be trying to answer?

......................................

......................................

......................................

**1.** ◉ **Text Features** Complete the chart to explain some of the features on this page.

| Feature | Clue |
|---------|------|
| heading | The heading tells that the paragraph is about questions. |
| picture | |

This scientist is studying cave formations.

## Investigations

Scientists do investigations to help them find answers to their questions. An **investigation** is a careful way of looking for something. Scientists use process skills in science investigations. You already use many of these skills in your daily life whenever you answer questions or solve problems. You will use them in a more organized way as you do science activities.

### Observe

Science often starts when a person observes something. For example, someone could visit a cave and observe the shapes of the cave walls. The person may then wonder how those shapes formed. Observations are made with the senses and with tools. Observations lead to questions that start an investigation. However, scientists continue making observations throughout an investigation.

### Research

After scientists ask a question, they do research by studying reference materials. Reference materials include encyclopedias, books, magazines or journals, the Internet, and more. Scientists often write articles that appear in scientific journals. Other scientists read the articles. This helps scientists learn what others have already discovered.

When scientists use information from a reference material, they keep track of where the information came from. They write down the name of the book or article and the name of the person who wrote it. It is important for others to be able to find the reference material the scientists used.

3. **Underline** the information you would need to write down about an article in a scientific journal.

4. **Apply** Look at the cave photos on this page. What research might you want to do before exploring a cave?

........................................................................................

........................................................................................

### Experiment

Scientists use their observations and research to come up with possible answers to their questions. Then they design and run tests to try to confirm those answers. These tests are called experiments. Scientists record their observations during experiments. The results of an experiment may match the earlier answer or provide a different answer. The results of their experiments are added to their earlier observations and research.

5. **Apply** What might you ask about the rock on this page? What experiment might you do to answer the question?

.................................................................................................

.................................................................................................

.................................................................................................

## Got it?

4.NS.1, 4.NS.4, 4.NS.6

6. **Ask Questions** What would you like to know about land features in your state? Write a question.

.................................................................................................

7. **Judge** Why might some reference materials be better than others?

.................................................................................................

8. **Infer** Why might scientists repeat experiments?

.................................................................................................

.................................................................................................

⬛ **Stop!** I need help with ..........................................................

⏸ **Wait!** I have a question about ..............................................

▶ **Go!** Now I know ....................................................................

## Lesson 2

# How do scientists use tools?

### Envision It!

4.NS.4 Perform investigations using appropriate tools and technology that will extend the senses.
4.NS.5 Use measurement skills and apply appropriate skills when collecting data.

**Circle** two tools that help you see things that are very small.

---

**Inquiry** **Explore It!**

## How can tools help you observe?

☑ 1. **Observe** a penny, a tissue, and a small rock using a hand lens.

☑ 2. Use a microscope to observe the penny and the tissue.

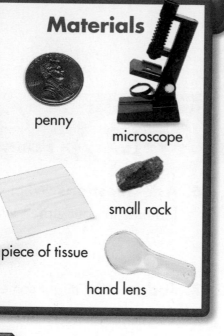

### Materials

penny

microscope

small rock

piece of tissue

hand lens

## Explain Your Results

3. **Draw a Conclusion** Which tool worked better for **observing** each object? Explain.

..................................................................................

..................................................................................

..................................................................................

..................................................................................

..................................................................................

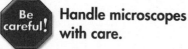 **Be careful!** **Handle microscopes with care.**

myscienceonline.com | **Explore It!** Animation

 4.NS.3 Plan and carry out investigations as a class, in small groups or independently, often over a period of several class lessons.

**Word to Know**

tool

## Tools

Scientists use many different kinds of tools. A **tool** is an object or device used to perform a task. The tool you use depends on the task. Tools can help you measure objects or gather information. You can measure volume, temperature, length, distance, mass, and more with the proper tools. Measurements give you exact observations that you can share with others. Scientists choose different tools based on how exact they need their measurements to be.

1. **Underline** two things that tools help you do.

2. **Infer** (Circle) the measurement that is more exact.
   about 5 cm
   5.3 cm

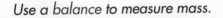

*Use a balance to measure mass.*

*Use a graduated cylinder to measure volume.*

*Use a metric ruler to measure length and distance.*

## More Tools

Tools can serve many purposes as you conduct science experiments and investigations. Some tools help with observations, helping you to see things that are very small or very far away in more detail.

Other tools such as a computer, can help analyze or visualize data. Computers with access to the Internet can help you find information collected by others. A computer can also help you create presentations to communicate your results to others.

*Use a hand lens to make objects appear larger. This allows you to see more detail than you could with just your eyes.*

3. **Apply** Use a hand lens to observe a leaf. Draw what you see.

*Use a telescope to help you see objects that are far away.*

4. **Compare** How is your drawing of a leaf like the drawings of others?

.................................................................

.................................................................

myscienceonline.com  I Will Know...

*Use a computer to analyze data.*

**5. Explain** Tell another way you use a computer.

*Microscopes use several lenses to make objects appear much larger. Use microscopes to see things in greater detail.*

**6. Apply** Tell what you would look at with a microscope.

*Use a thermometer to measure temperature.*

## Compare Observations

Scientists make observations many times to make sure their data are accurate. Data are the facts you collect as you observe. Scientists record their findings, and then compare their data with the observations of other scientists. Even though groups of scientists may use different tools to observe, their data should be similar.

Comparing your results with others is important. Sometimes there are errors in how observations are made. Sometimes the tool being used has a flaw. Sometimes a scientist misses an important detail.

**7. ◉ Text Features** Why do you think some of the words in the captions are purple?

........................................................................

........................................................................

**8. Infer** Why do you think people with long hair need to tie it back when they do a science experiment?

...................................................

...................................................

...................................................

**9. Identify** Suppose you are doing an activity with vinegar and baking soda. (Circle) the safety rules that apply.

## Safety

Scientists know that they must work safely when doing experiments and using tools. You need to be careful when you do science activities too. Always follow these safety rules.

### Science Safety Rules

- Read the activity carefully before you start.
- Listen to the teacher's instructions. Ask questions about things you do not understand.
- Keep your work area neat and clean. Clean up spills right away.
- Never taste or smell any substance unless directed to do so by your teacher.
- Handle sharp items and other equipment carefully.
- Use chemicals carefully. Dispose of chemicals properly.
- Help keep plants and animals that you use safe.
- Tell your teacher if there is an accident or if you see anything that looks unsafe.
- Wash your hands well when you are finished.
- Wear safety goggles and gloves when necessary.
- Tie back long hair.

**10. Explain** What do these students need to do to be safe?

...................................................

...................................................

Following safety rules keeps you and others safe from getting hurt. Some chemicals can damage your skin or eyes. Safety goggles and gloves can protect you from these chemicals. If you are working with something that is sharp or moves quickly, safety goggles will protect your eyes. Gloves can protect your hands.

**11. Write** The students below are following safety rules. Explain how each student is protected.

## Got it?

4.NS.4, 4.NS.5

**12. Summarize** How can tools help you do science?

........................................................................................

........................................................................................

**13.** UNLOCK THE BIG **Judge** Why is it important for scientists to compare their observations with the observations of others?

........................................................................................

........................................................................................

........................................................................................

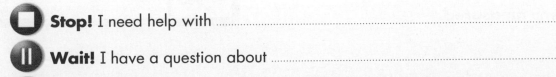

⬛ **Stop!** I need help with ................................................................

⏸ **Wait!** I have a question about ..................................................

▶ **Go!** Now I know ........................................................................

## Lesson 3

# How do scientists answer questions?

4.NS.2 Design a fair test. 4.NS.6 Test predictions with multiple trials. 4.NS.9 Compare the results of an investigation with the prediction.

## Envision It!

**Tell** what question you have about the starfish.

## Inquiry  Explore It!

### What helps scientists answer questions?

Scientists try to find answers to questions by following certain principles. In an investigation, they change only one thing, measure how something else changes, and keep everything else the same. Think about these principles as you try to answer this question: How does temperature affect how much salt dissolves?

☑ **1.** To a cup of cold water, add 1 level spoonful of salt and stir until it dissolves. Repeat until the salt no longer dissolves. **Record** how many spoonfuls you added before it stopped dissolving.

☑ **2.** Repeat Step 1 but change from cold water to warm water.

### Explain Your Results

**3.** Identify the one thing you changed.

**4.** Identify what you **measured.**

**5.** Identify one thing you made sure not to change.

### Materials

plastic cup of very cold water
plastic cup of warm water

salt          spoon

### Data Table

|  | **Number of Spoonfuls of Salt** |
|---|---|
| **Cold Water** |  |
| **Warm Water** |  |

myscienceonline.com | Explore It! Animation

4.NS.7 Keep accurate records in a notebook during investigations and communicate findings to others using graphs, charts, maps and models through oral and written reports. (Also 4.NS.3)

I will know some different
scientific methods scientists
use to answer questions.

**Words to Know**

scientific methods
hypothesis
evidence
three-dimensional
two-dimensional

**Tell** how you could find an answer to your question.

## Scientific Methods

Scientists use scientific methods as they work. Scientific
methods are organized ways to answer questions and
solve problems. Scientific methods help scientists draw
conclusions. Scientists do not always use the same methods.
They do not follow the methods in rigid order. Scientists
record their method so it can be repeated accurately. You
will use scientific methods when you do experiments.

Scientific methods include experiments, observations,
surveys, and sampling. In a survey, scientists ask people
a number of questions and then analyze the answers. A
survey might help scientists find the source of an illness,
for example. Sampling is another way of collecting data.
Scientists may take samples of a population. They might
catch, test, and release birds to see if they are healthy.

1. **Underline** the definition of *scientific methods*.

2. **Evaluate** Cross out the statement that is
   not true.

   Surveys are one type of
   scientific method.

   The scientific method follows a
   rigid order.

   Scientists make careful observations.

**3. Ask Questions**

Suppose the scientist in
the picture below wants
to see how petrels care
for their young. What
scientific methods can
she use to answer her
question?

.................................................

.................................................

*This scientist studies the
habits of petrels.*

# A Bouncing-Ball Experiment

Science begins with an observation. For example, you may notice that a ball bounces differently in different rooms. These two pages show a series of steps that can be used to design and conduct a bouncing-ball experiment.

## Ask a question.

You might have a question about something you observe.

*How high will the ball bounce on different surfaces?*

## State your hypothesis.

A **hypothesis** is a possible answer to your question. It often predicts an outcome of an experiment. Write it as an *If . . . then . . . because . . .* statement.

*If I drop the ball, then it will bounce highest on the rubber mat, because the rubber mat is the most flexible.*

## Identify and control variables.

Variables are things that can change. For a fair test, choose just one variable to change. Keep the other variables the same.

In this experiment there are 3 types of variables. The *independent variable* is the thing that you change. In this experiment, the surface is the independent variable. The thing that you must measure or observe is the *dependent variable*. Here, the dependent variable is how high the ball bounces. Controlled variables are things you keep the same so they do not affect the dependent variable.

*Test other surfaces. Bounce the ball off of wood, carpet, and a rubber mat.*

4. **Identify** What are some of the controlled variables?

..................................................................................

..................................................................................

..................................................................................

 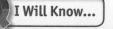

## Test your hypothesis.

Make a plan to test your hypothesis. Collect materials and tools. Then follow your plan. Each time you test a surface is called a trial. Repeat each trial three times.

## Collect and record your data.

Keep good records of what you do and find out. Use tables and pictures to help.

## Interpret your data.

Organize your notes and records to make them clear. Make diagrams, charts, or graphs to help.

## State your conclusion.

Your conclusion is a decision you make based on your data. Communicate what you found out. Tell whether your data supported your hypothesis.

*The data did not support my hypothesis. The ball bounced highest when dropped onto the piece of wood.*

## Try it again.

Do the experiment a few more times. The results of one experiment might not be right. Be sure to do everything exactly the same each time.

---

5. **Generate** Write a new hypothesis about how high the ball will bounce on different surfaces.

.............................................

.............................................

.............................................

.............................................

.............................................

.............................................

6. ◎ **Text Features** Why are pictures shown with some of the steps?

.............................................

.............................................

.............................................

.............................................

7. **Predict** Tell how the outcome of the experiment might change when the experiment is repeated.

.............................................

.............................................

.............................................

.............................................

## Creativity

Scientists have to be creative when designing experiments. They need to think of ways to control variables so trials are the same. They need to think of what might go wrong. Think about the bouncing ball experiment. What if the scientist only said to drop the ball from a table? Other scientists may not have tables that are the same height. Some scientists might push the ball off the table and others might just let it drop. These could lead to different results. Using a meterstick to measure the exact height eliminates the differences created by using a table.

8. CHALLENGE Sometimes tests like this are done by dropping the ball inside a clear plastic tube. How would that make the experiment better and how could it make it worse?

.......................................................................................

.......................................................................................

.......................................................................................

# Observation and Evidence

Scientists make careful observations to find answers to their questions. Taking measurements is one way scientists can make observations. Scientists use evidence to decide whether their hypotheses are correct. Observations and facts gained from experiments are **evidence.**

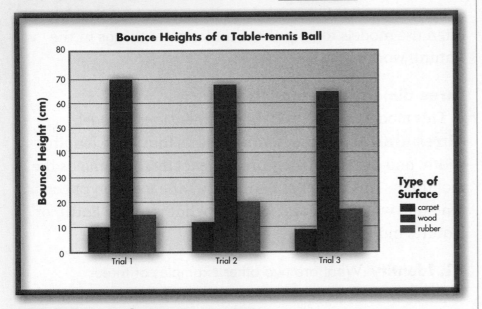

**Bounce Heights of a Table-tennis Ball**

## Estimates and Measurements

Scientists often make estimates. They tell what they think an object's size, mass, or temperature will measure. Then they measure these factors in units. Scientists usually measure in metric units. The United States commonly uses non-metric units such as gallons, pounds, and inches.

## Multiple Trials

A single trial may not give an accurate result. Because of this, scientists perform multiple trials during an experiment. When all the results are gathered together, patterns should develop. How many trials to perform depends on what you are trying to test. For example, the chart above shows results from three trials. Notice that all the heights in the trials are different. If you were testing the exact height a ball would bounce on a surface, you should complete several trials.

**9. Exemplify** What would you observe in the bouncing-ball experiment?

...............................

...............................

...............................

...............................

...............................

...............................

...............................

**10. Analyze** Do three trials give enough evidence to show which surface makes the ball bounce highest? Why or why not?

...............................

...............................

...............................

...............................

...............................

...............................

...............................

## Models

Sometimes scientists want to test things they cannot test on actual objects. For example, a scientist may want to know how strong winds affect an airplane. The scientist can test a model of the plane using a wind tunnel. Models are objects or ideas that represent other things. They may show how something is made or how it works. Scientists often use models to help them understand things in the natural world.

### Three-dimensional models

This model of Earth is a three-dimensional model. **Three-dimensional** describes objects that have length, width, and height. Models are not exactly the same as the real thing. This model of Earth shows the location of Earth's land and water but does not show what is inside Earth, or features made by people.

**11. Identify** What are two other examples of three-dimensional models?

This is the largest moving model of Earth in the world.

### Two-dimensional models

Some models are two-dimensional. **Two-dimensional** describes something that has length and width but not height. Two-dimensional models are flat. A map is an example of a two-dimensional model.

**12. Produce** Draw a two-dimensional model of your classroom.

The World

## Explanations

After scientists design their experiments and run trials, they use evidence to explain the results. The explanation should answer the original question the experiment was designed to ask. The explanation will also tell whether the hypothesis was supported by data. An important thing to remember is that a hypothesis is a possible answer to the question. It is based on the best information you have at the time, but if your results do not support the hypothesis, an experiment is not a failure. It still gives information about the question.

13. **Summarize** What was the hypothesis in the bouncing-ball experiment? Did the data support the hypothesis?

......................................................................................

......................................................................................

......................................................................................

### At-Home Lab

**Trial Testing**
Test how high a table-tennis ball will bounce on concrete. Use the procedure from the bouncing-ball experiment. Record your data. Be sure to do multiple trials. Compare your data with others. Explain why the data might be different. Draw a conclusion.

## Got it?

🕐 4.NS.2, 4.NS.7, 4.NS.9

14. **Summarize** Name three methods scientists might use to investigate a question or problem.

......................................................................................

......................................................................................

15. **UNLOCK THE BIG Q** Why do you think evidence is important in science?

......................................................................................

......................................................................................

......................................................................................

⬛ **Stop!** I need help with ..........................................................

⏸ **Wait!** I have a question about .................................................

▶ **Go!** Now I know ....................................................................

## Lesson 4
# How do scientists draw conclusions?

**4.NS.7** Keep accurate records in a notebook during investigations and communicate findings to others using graphs, charts, maps and models through oral and written reports. **4.NS.8** Identify simple patterns in data and propose explanations to account for the patterns. **4.NS.9** Compare the results of an investigation with the prediction.

## Envision It!

**Tell** what you think this scientist is writing down.

## Inquiry Explore It!

### How can you record data?

☑ **1.** Put the paper clips in a cup. Dip a magnet into the cup. Pull it out. Count the paper clips it picked up. Use the chart to **record** your **data.** Record your data in another way by using a bar graph.

☑ **2.** Repeat your trials 2 more times. Record.

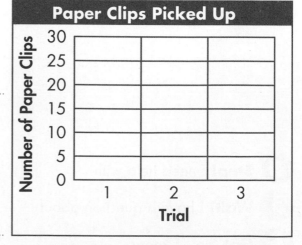

**Materials**

magnet

paper clips

plastic cup

| Paper Clips Picked Up | |
|---|---|
| Trial | Number |
| 1 | |
| 2 | |
| 3 | |

### Explain Your Results

**3. Communicate** Compare the **records** of your **data** with the records made by other groups.

**4. Draw a Conclusion** Based on the data you recorded, how many paper clips is your magnet able to pick up? How did the data help you draw your conclusion?

**Paper Clips Picked Up**

Number of Paper Clips: 30, 25, 20, 15, 10, 5, 0

Trial: 1, 2, 3

myscienceonline.com | Explore It! Animation

**4.NS.6** Test predictions with multiple trials. **4.NS.7** Keep accurate records in a notebook during investigations and communicate findings to others using graphs, charts, maps and models through oral and written reports. (Also **4.NS.3**, **4.DP.9**)

I will know how scientists keep records in order to share conclusions with other scientists.

**Words to Know**
...............................

procedure
inference

## Record Procedures

The bouncing-ball experiment from the previous lesson identifies different variables to test the hypothesis. How can other scientists use the experiment to get their own results? How can you use the results to draw conclusions?

The scientist in the photo above is keeping records of underwater observations. Scientists must also carefully record how they performed experiments in procedures. A **procedure** is a set of step-by-step instructions for how to perform a test. When you write a procedure, be sure to be clear. This allows others to repeat the test to get similar results. When repeating an experiment, it is important to do a test exactly the same way each time.

1. **Analyze** What might happen if a procedure is not clearly written?

........................................................

........................................................

........................................................

**Question:** A table-tennis ball will bounce highest on which surface?

**Hypothesis:** If I drop the ball, then it will bounce highest on the rubber mat, because the rubber mat is the most flexible.

**Materials:** table-tennis ball, piece of wood, rubber mat, piece of carpet, meterstick

**Procedure:**
1. Place the piece of wood on the floor. Hold the meterstick upright on the wood.

2. Drop the table-tennis ball from a height of 1 meter onto the wood. Be careful not to push or throw the ball down.

3. Record how high the ball bounces.

4. Repeat Steps 1–3 using the rubber mat.

5. Repeat Steps 1–3 using the piece of carpet.

6. Repeat the entire experiment 2 more times.

## Keep Records

By keeping detailed and accurate records of observations, scientists are able to share their information with others. The more scientists repeat an experiment and get the same results, the more they can rely on the data. Conclusions based on reliable data are more likely to continue to be useful in the future. For example, think of the diver on the previous page. If the records of the dive are accurate, scientists can look for more or different information on future dives.

Scientists continue to repeat an experiment until they are sure of the results. If scientists repeat an experiment and get different results, they look for reasons why the experiment was different. Good records and procedures can be helpful in finding those reasons.

## Organize Your Data

Scientists keep accurate records of their experiments. Often they organize their data in a table. The table below contains important information about the bouncing-ball experiment. The title explains what was tested. The table names the materials used and gives the test results. The table also shows that the experiment was done three times.

2. ⊙ **Text Features** What information does the table give you?

............................

............................

............................

3. **Conclude** Make a conclusion based on the data. Which surface caused the ball to bounce highest?

............................

............................

............................

............................

| Bounce Heights of a Table-tennis Ball | | | |
|---|---|---|---|
| Material | Bounce Height (cm) | | |
| | Trial 1 | Trial 2 | Trial 3 |
| Carpet | 10 | 12 | 9 |
| Wood | 70 | 68 | 65 |
| Rubber | 15 | 20 | 17 |

# Presenting Data

There are many different formats for organizing and arranging your data. The table on the previous page is one format. Charts and graphs can also be helpful because they show information in a way that is easy to understand. However you format your data, it should be clearly labled.

## Bar graph

A bar graph uses rectangular bars to compare data. The bars may be vertical or horizontal. The bars often have different colors or shading for each variable.

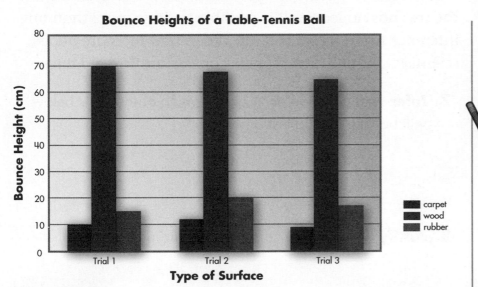

**Bounce Heights of a Table-Tennis Ball**

## Line graph

Line graphs connect points of data on a graph with straight lines. Line graphs are often used to show patterns of data over time. For example, a line graph could show the amount of rainfall a place gets over two weeks. A graph may use different colored lines to compare different data.

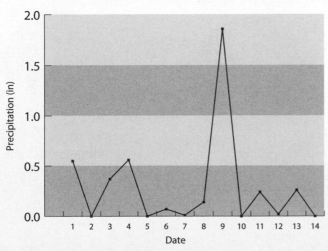

Daily Precipitation, Dallas-Ft. Worth Airport, October 2009

**4. Conclude** In the bar graph shown here, what would happen if the color key was missing?

.......................

.......................

.......................

.......................

**5. Express Data** Work with a partner to write a 1–2 sentence explanation of the data in the line graph. Read your explanation.

.......................

.......................

.......................

.......................

.......................

.......................

## Evidence and Inferences

Scientists base their explanations on evidence. Evidence includes any information you have and observations that you make. An observation from an experiment is a piece of evidence. Facts you already have, or research you have done, are also evidence.

Scientists use evidence to make inferences. An **inference** is a conclusion drawn from data and observations. For example, the statement *The tree has no leaves on it* is an observation. *The tree lost its leaves because the season is fall* is an inference. It is a conclusion drawn from the fact that the tree has no leaves. It is possible to draw more than one inference from the same data. When new facts are added, scientists can draw new conclusions or confirm old ones.

**6. Infer** Someone noticed that a tree had no leaves and inferred that it lost its leaves because the season is fall. Write another reasonable inference based on this observation.

**7. Infer** Make an inference about which of the balls below will bounce the highest on wood.

.............................................................

.............................................................

**8. Justify** What evidence supports your inference?

.............................................................

.............................................................

.............................................................

fabric ball    golf ball    table-tennis ball

## Reasonable Answers

Scientists attempt to develop reasonable answers to the questions they pose. To do this, they use evidence from their observations and experiments. For the bouncing-ball experiment, you would use evidence gathered by doing the procedure from the previous pages. A reasonable answer should not favor one opinion over another unless it is supported by evidence.

## Compare Results

Scientists often compare their methods or procedures with those of their peers. They also compare their results. By comparing methods and results, scientists can work to find results that can be retested.

In the bouncing-ball experiment, one group can compare their results with another group. The scientists determine whether the results are similar or different. They try to explain why the results are similar or different. Scientists often do this to think of new questions or better ways to perform a test.

9. **Decide** Why is it important to compare results with others?

..................................................................................................

..................................................................................................

..................................................................................................

..................................................................................................

**Lightning Lab**

**Observations and Inferences**
Examine a coin. List everything you can about the coin that is factual. Next, make some inferences about the coin or the country that minted it. Compare your lists of facts and inferences with those of your classmates.

plastic foam ball

rubber ball

## Go Further

Once an experiment is complete, scientists use what they learn. The results of an experiment can become part of the background research other scientists use for future experiments. An experiment may lead to new questions to test. Scientists may also think of better ways to do a test.

**10. Formulate** Suppose you wanted to get a more precise measurement of how high the ball would bounce on wood. How would you change the experiment?

..................................................................

..................................................................

Think back to the bouncing-ball experiment. The original question was how high a ball would bounce on different surfaces. The hypothesis was that a rubber surface would make the ball bounce higher. The conclusion was a wood surface made the ball bounce higher. The completed experiment might raise questions about how other surfaces would affect the ball. Or it may raise questions about the ball itself. Does the ball bounce differently if it is hot or cold? How might it bounce compared to other balls?

**11. Revise** Suppose you wanted to perform three trials to test how high a ball bounced if it was at a cooler temperature. How might you organize your results? Complete the table below. (Circle) the independent variables in the completed table.

**12. Predict** This scientist is testing a pesticide on plants in a laboratory. When this experiment is complete, how might it lead to a new experiment?

..................................................................

..................................................................

..................................................................

..................................................................

| Bounce Heights at Different Temperatures | | | |
|---|---|---|---|
|  |  |  |  |
|  |  |  |  |
|  |  |  |  |
|  |  |  |  |

# Do the math!

## Interpret Data

Three different students tried the experiment with the table-tennis ball. They tested materials to see which caused the ball to bounce highest. The chart shows their results.

| Bounce Heights of a Table-tennis Ball | | | |
|---|---|---|---|
| Material | Bounce Height (cm) | | |
| | Student A | Student B | Student C |
| Carpet | 7 | 12 | 6 |
| Wood | 70 | 73 | 65 |
| Rubber | 12 | 20 | 13 |

**1** What might account for the different results?

............................................................

............................................................

............................................................

**2** What question were students trying to answer? What can they conclude?

............................................................

............................................................

............................................................

............................................................

## Got it?

🕐 **4.NS.6, 4.NS.8**

13. ⊙ **Compare and Contrast** How is evidence different from an inference?

............................................................

............................................................

14. **Evaluate** Why is it important to do an experiment the same way each time?

............................................................

■ **Stop!** I need help with ............................................................

❚❚ **Wait!** I have a question about ............................................................

▶ **Go!** Now I know ............................................................

# What affects how many times a pendulum swings?

## Follow a Procedure

☑ **1.** Set up a pendulum system.

☑ **2. Identify variables** that might change how many times the pendulum swings in 15 seconds. Use the materials you have. Make a list with other groups.

...................................................

...................................................

...................................................

...................................................

☑ **3.** Choose a variable to investigate. What variable did you choose?

...................................................

...................................................

...................................................

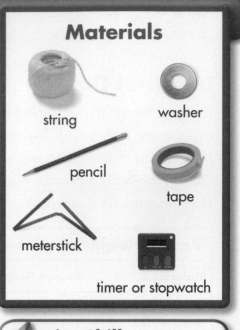

**Materials**

string

washer

pencil

tape

meterstick

timer or stopwatch

**Inquiry Skill**
Record your data on a chart. This can help you make **inferences** based on the data.

**4.DP.2** Brainstorm potential solutions. **4.DP.9** Present evidence using mathematical representations (graphs, data tables). (Also **4.NS.2**, **4.NS.7**)

**4.** Swing the pendulum. **Measure** the number of swings in 15 seconds. **Record** on the chart.

**5.** Change the value of your variable. Repeat Step 4.

| Observations of Pendulum Swings | |
| --- | --- |
| Variable: _____ | Number of Swings in 15 seconds |
| | |
| | |
| | |
| | |

## Analyze and Conclude

**6. Communicate** Compare your results with other groups. Which variable had the greatest effect on the pendulum?

........................................................................................

........................................................................................

**7. UNLOCK THE BIG Q Infer** How did scientific methods help you during your investigation?

........................................................................................

........................................................................................

........................................................................................

# Otis Boykin

🔵 4.NS.1

Some people have a heart disease that causes their hearts to beat either too quickly or too slowly. Scientists identified the problem and started working on a solution. The solution was the pacemaker. This small electronic device sends electric pulses to the heart. It keeps the heart beating at the proper rhythm. One part of the pacemaker was invented by Otis Boykin. Boykin's part controlled the amount of electricity given off by the pacemaker.

As an inventor, Otis Boykin used scientific methods to test his inventions. Inventors make things that solve problems. They ask questions, make observations, and do experiments.

Otis Boykin grew up in Dallas, Texas. He graduated from Fisk University in Nashville, Tennessee. Then he worked in Chicago, Illinois. It was not long before he began inventing. He invented electrical devices used in guided missiles and in computers. Altogether, Boykin invented twenty-six electrical devices.

**APPLY THE BIG ?** In what ways do you think Boykin used science in his career?

pacemaker

Otis Boykin
(1920–1982)

# Vocabulary Smart Cards

inquiry
investigation
tool
scientific methods
hypothesis
evidence
three-dimensional
two-dimensional
procedure
inference

## Play a Game!

Cut out the Vocabulary Smart Cards.

Work with a partner. Choose a Vocabulary Smart Card.

Say as many words as you can think of that are related to that vocabulary word in some way.

Have your partner guess the word.

**scientific methods**

métodos científicos

**inquiry**

indagación

**hypothesis**

hipótesis

**investigation**

investigación

**evidence**

Bounce Heights of a Table-Tennis Ball

Bounce Height (cm)

Trial 1    Trial 2    Trial 3

Type of Surface

evidencia

**tool**

instrumento

35

the process of asking questions and searching for answers

Write a sentence using the verb form of this word.

................................................

................................................

................................................

proceso que consiste en preguntar y buscar respuestas

organized ways to answer questions and solve problems

Write two examples.

................................................

................................................

................................................

maneras organizadas de responder a preguntas y resolver problemas

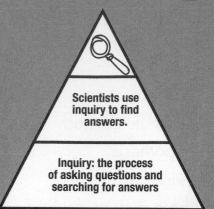

Scientists use inquiry to find answers.

Inquiry: the process of asking questions and searching for answers

## Make a Word Pyramid!

Choose a vocabulary word and write the definition in the base of the pyramid. Write a sentence in the middle of the pyramid. Draw a picture of an example, or of something related, at the top.

a careful way of looking for something

Write three related words.

................................................

................................................

................................................

................................................

manera cuidadosa de buscar algo

a possible answer to a question

Write a sentence using this word.

................................................

................................................

................................................

................................................

respuesta posible a una pregunta

an object or device used to perform a task

Draw an example.

objeto o herramienta que se usa para hacer un trabajo

observations and facts gained from experiments

Write a sentence using this term.

................................................

................................................

................................................

observaciones y datos obtenidos de experimentos

inference

inferencia

three-dimensional

tridimensional

two-dimensional

bidimensional

procedure

**Question:** A table-tennis ball will bounce highest on which surface?

**Hypothesis:** If I drop the ball, then it will bounce highest on the rubber mat, because the rubber mat is the most flexible.

**Materials:** table-tennis ball, piece of wood, rubber mat, piece of carpet, meterstick

**Procedure:**
1. Place the piece of wood on the floor. Hold the meterstick upright on the wood.
2. Drop the table-tennis ball from a height of 1 meter onto the wood. Be careful not to push or throw the ball down.
3. Record how high the ball bounces.
4. Repeat Steps 1–3 using the rubber mat.
5. Repeat Steps 1–3 using the piece of carpet.
6. Repeat the entire experiment 2 more times.

procedimiento

describes objects that have length, width, and height

Write three examples.

........................................

........................................

........................................

........................................

describe objetos que tienen largo, ancho y altura

---

a conclusion drawn from data and observations

Write a sentence using the verb form of this word.

........................................

........................................

........................................

........................................

conclusión que se saca de los datos y de las observaciones

---

describes something that has length and width, but not height

Draw an example.

describe algo que tiene largo y ancho, pero no tiene altura

---

........................................

........................................

........................................

---

........................................

........................................

........................................

---

a set of step-by-step instructions

Write three related words.

........................................

........................................

........................................

........................................

instrucciones paso por paso

---

........................................

........................................

........................................

---

........................................

........................................

........................................

# Study Guide

 **What is science?**

**Lesson 1**

### What questions do scientists ask?

- Scientists ask questions about the natural world.
- Scientists observe and do research while conducting investigations.
- Scientists develop hypotheses based on collected data.

**Lesson 2**

### How do scientists use tools?

- A tool is an object or device used to perform a task.
- Scientists use many tools, including thermometers, microscopes, pan balances, and computers.

**Lesson 3**

### How do scientists answer questions?

- Scientific methods are organized steps for doing an investigation.
- Evidence is used to develop reasonable answers to questions.
- Scientists compare their results with other scientists' results.

**Lesson 4**

### How do scientists draw conclusions?

- Procedures are step-by-step instructions for how to perform tests.
- Scientists keep detailed and accurate records in order to share their findings with others.

## Lesson 1   4.NS.1

**What questions do scientists ask?**

1. **Vocabulary** Inquiry is the process of_____
   A. doing work.
   B. asking questions.
   C. analyzing data.
   D. reporting results.

2. **Explain** How can scientists develop explanations about data?

..............................................................

..............................................................

..............................................................

..............................................................

..............................................................

3. **Ask Questions** A team of scientists is studying the formation of islands in the Pacific Ocean. Provide a question that the team might ask.

..............................................................

..............................................................

..............................................................

..............................................................

## Lesson 2   4.NS.4, 4.NS.5

**How do scientists use tools?**

**Measurement Long Ago**
   Long ago, people measured by using familiar objects. They used a forearm or a foot to measure length. For smaller measurements, they might have used the width of a man's thumb. They measured weight with stones or even with seeds from different plants.

4. **Text Features** What does the heading in the passage above tell you?

..............................................................

..............................................................

..............................................................

5. **Recognize** A graduated cylinder is used to measure_____
   A. temperature.
   B. mass.
   C. volume.
   D. weight.

6. **Explain** Why do scientists use tools to measure things and gather information?

..............................................................

..............................................................

..............................................................

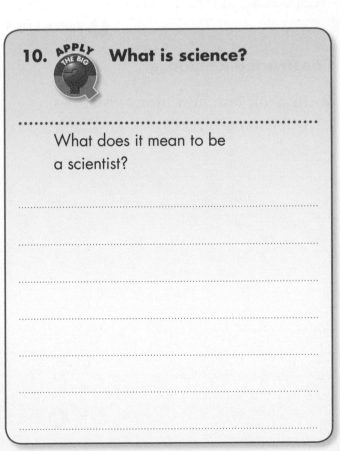

## Lesson 3   4.NS.2, 4.NS.8

### How do scientists answer questions?

7. **Summarize** What are some of the organized steps that scientists use to answer questions and solve problems?

8. **Evaluate** In an experiment, the thing you are trying to measure or observe is the _____
A. controlled variable.
B. dependent variable.
C. independent variable.
D. hypothesis.

## Lesson 4   4.NS.7, 4.NS.8, 4.NS.9

### How do scientists draw conclusions?

9. **Apply** Why do scientists keep detailed and accurate records?

10. **APPLY THE BIG Q** What is science?

What does it mean to be a scientist?

## Multiple Choice

**1** Which of these is not a measuring tool?

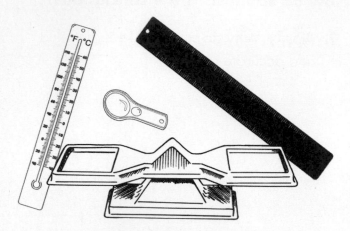

A. a thermometer

B. a pan balance

C. a meterstick

D. a hand lens

**🕐 4.NS.4, 4.NS.5**

## Constructed Response

**2** In a fair test, how many variables will change?

.....................................................................

.....................................................................

.....................................................................

.....................................................................

.....................................................................

.....................................................................

**🕐 4.NS.2**

## Extended Response

**3** Study the item below, then answer the following questions.

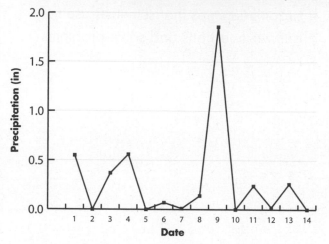

Daily Precipitation, Dallas-Ft. Worth Airport, October 2009

What kind of graph is shown above?

.....................................................................

.....................................................................

Examine the data pattern in the graph. What might you infer from the graph about the precipitation in Dallas-Fort Worth?

.....................................................................

.....................................................................

How could you improve your data to test your inference above?

.....................................................................

**🕐 4.NS.7, 4.NS.8**

# Indiana's Plants

4.NS.4, 4.NS.7

You can practice the skill of observation by carefully examining an Indiana plant. Go outside with an adult and a notebook. Bring a hand lens if you like. Find a plant that interests you. It can be in a garden, or it can be growing wild. Do not touch the plant. Observe the plant carefully. Draw the plant. Then write down observations about how it looks.

**Illustrate** Draw the plant.

Record observations about how it looks.

Use reference materials from your school media center to identify the plant. Write down the name of the plant and the title of the reference material you used.

# What can you test in a wind tunnel?

# Technology and Design

**Try It!** How can you make a paper helicopter drop slowly?

**Lesson 1** What is technology?
4.DP.1, 4.4.1

**Lesson 2** What is the design process?
4.DP.4, 4.DP.5, 4.DP.10, 4.4.1

**Investigate It!** Which boat design will hold more cargo?

Scientists and engineers use wind tunnels to test how air moves around cars, planes, people, or other objects. The smoother the air flows around an object the faster the object can travel and the less energy it will need to move.

**Predict** What can a downhill skier learn from wind tunnel tests? Explain your answer.

........................................................................

........................................................................

........................................................................

........................................................................

**THE BIG Q** How does technology affect our lives?

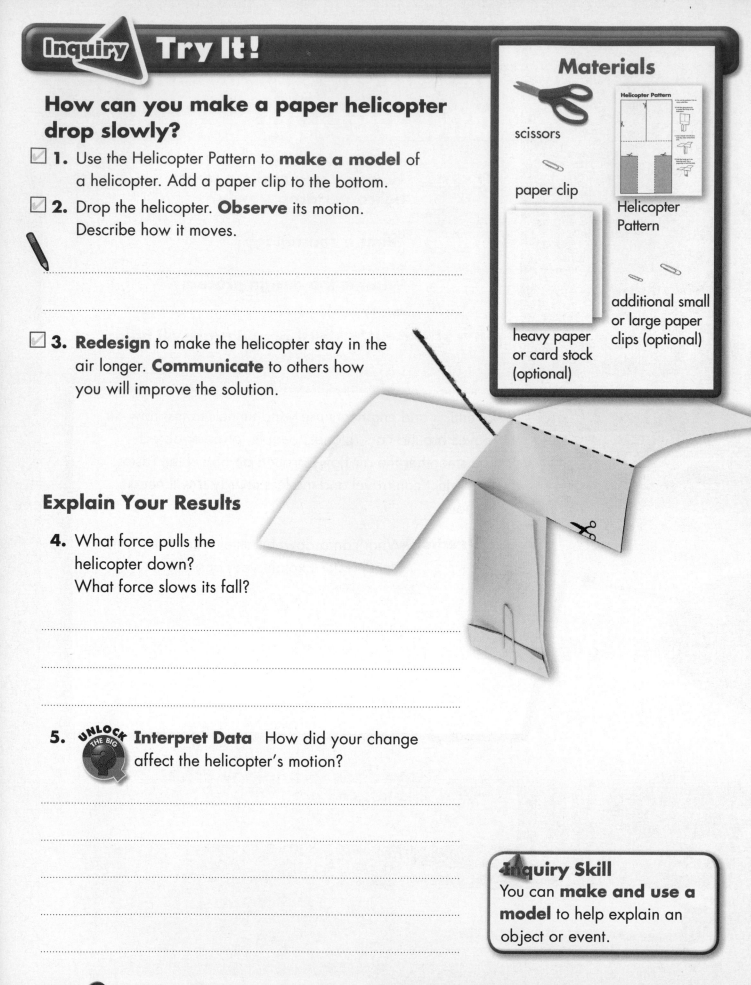

# Inquiry ▶ Try It!

## How can you make a paper helicopter drop slowly?

☑ **1.** Use the Helicopter Pattern to **make a model** of a helicopter. Add a paper clip to the bottom.

☑ **2.** Drop the helicopter. **Observe** its motion. Describe how it moves.

...................................................................

...................................................................

☑ **3. Redesign** to make the helicopter stay in the air longer. **Communicate** to others how you will improve the solution.

### Materials

scissors

paper clip

heavy paper or card stock (optional)

Helicopter Pattern

additional small or large paper clips (optional)

## Explain Your Results

**4.** What force pulls the helicopter down? What force slows its fall?

...................................................................

...................................................................

...................................................................

**5.** **UNLOCK THE BIG Q** **Interpret Data** How did your change affect the helicopter's motion?

...................................................................

...................................................................

...................................................................

...................................................................

> **Inquiry Skill**
> You can **make and use a model** to help explain an object or event.

**4.DP.1** Identify a need or problem to be solved. **4.DP.7** Test and evaluate how well the solution meets the goal. **4.DP.11** Communicate how to improve the solution. (Also **4.4.1**, **4.4.3**, **4.DP.10**)

# Cause and Effect

- A **cause** is why something happens.
- An **effect** is what happens.
- When you read, sometimes clue words such as *because* and *since* indicate a relationship of cause and effect.

## Rubber Tires

Before the 1800s, wheels were made of wood and metal. A thin metal tire was wrapped around a wood rim. Riding in a vehicle with these rigid tires was very bumpy. Because of this, some inventors decided to use rubber to make tires. The flexibility of rubber made the ride less bumpy. Today, rubber tires are used on bikes, cars, tractors, and trucks.

# Practice It!

Use the graphic organizer below to list one cause and one effect found in the example paragraph.

**Cause**

**Effect**

myscienceonline.com | **Vocabulary Smart Cards**

47

# Lesson 1

# What is technology?

4.4.1 Investigate transportation systems and devices that operate on or in land, water, air and space and recognize the forces (lift, drag, friction, thrust and gravity) that affect their motion. (Also 4.DP.1)

## Envision It!

**Tell** what problem this communications satellite might help solve.

## my planet diary *for* Indiana

Ray Harroun's 1911 racecar

Side-view mirror

Rear-view camera in automobile

## Connections

Sometimes adding older technology to something new can help solve problems. The first Indianapolis 500 automobile race was held in 1911. Racecars at the time carried two people. A mechanic would ride with the driver. The mechanic would fix the car and warn the driver about cars behind them.

Driver Ray Harroun was also an automobile designer. He designed a racecar with room for only one person. To see behind the car, Harroun attached a mirror above the steering wheel. It became the first known rear-view mirror on an automobile. Driving without a mechanic was risky, but it paid off. Harroun became the first Indy 500 winner.

Cars today are still built with rear-view and side-view mirrors. However, there is new technology to help drivers know what is around them. Some cars use video cameras so drivers can see behind them. Some cars have sensors in the bumpers. Sounds or computerized voices may signal the driver if a car is too close to a curb.

What other technologies can improve a car's safety?

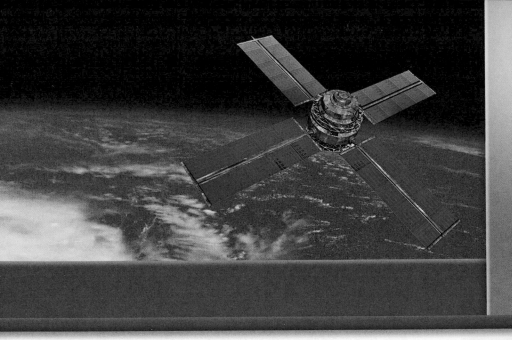

UNLOCK THE BIG ?

I will know how technology solves problems and makes work easier.

**Word to Know**

technology

## Scientific Discoveries

Scientific discoveries change our lives. The discovery of bacteria helped us develop modern medicine. Discoveries about how electricity works brought us telephones, computers, refrigerators, light bulbs, and many more devices. Scientific discoveries often lead to new technologies. **Technology** is the knowledge, processes, and products that solve problems and make work easier.

Just as scientific methods are used to answer scientific questions, people often use a process to design technology. This process involves identifying a problem, researching and testing possible solutions, and then redesigning if necessary.

*This smartphone combines many technologies into one device. The icons on the screen show some of its functions.*

1. **Underline** the definition of technology.

2. ◉ **Cause and Effect** Write one cause and effect related to technology.

| Cause | Effect |
| --- | --- |
|  | |

3. **Identify** What do you think people can do with a smartphone in addition to making phone calls?

....................................

....................................

....................................

....................................

The steam engine used steam from boiling water to move parts of machines. Steam engines were soon used to move vehicles.

Trains running on steam power were common from the 1800s into the mid-1900s.

A diesel-electric train burns a type of gasoline to power its engine. The diesel speed record is 238 kilometers per hour.

Magnetic levitation trains use powerful magnets to move just above their tracks.

**4. Predict** Many large cities have problems with heavy traffic. What technology might be developed in the future to help solve this problem?

## Technology and Transportation Systems

Transportation systems move people and goods from place to place. Technology has made transportation systems faster and safer. Long trips that once took days or weeks may now take only hours.

During the 1700s, steam engines were being developed. They first were used to operate machines in factories and mines. The invention of the steam engine led to many other technologies, such as the steam-powered train. The first steam-powered train traveled only about 6 kilometers per hour. As people developed better steam-powered trains, the trains could travel much faster.

**5. Give Examples** What are some other transportation systems?

Steam trains had some disadvantages. Water was heated inside a boiler, changing the water to steam. As the water changed to steam, pressure would build up inside the boiler. Sometimes the heat inside the boiler would melt a hole in the steel. The sudden release of steam out of the hole would cause the boiler to explode.

Electric, diesel, and magnetic levitation trains have replaced steam-powered trains. These trains are safer since they do not have a boiler that could explode. These trains are also faster. Magnetic levitation trains can reach speeds of more than 500 kilometers per hour.

GPS device

GPS technology keeps track of this city bus's location.

Today's transportation systems often use computer technology. Computers keep systems running properly and on time. Global Positioning System (GPS) technology sends location data from satellites orbiting Earth. A driver using a GPS device can get directions to a destination. Some city bus systems now have GPS in their buses. People waiting for a bus can use cell phones to find out if their bus is running on time.

**6. Apply** What is another problem a GPS device might solve?

........................................

........................................

........................................

........................................

## Everyday Technologies

You may be surprised at the technology you can find in your home or at school. Can openers, microwave ovens, refrigerators, windows, pens, computers, clocks, and microphones are all technologies.

**Technology at Home**

In the past, people would have to eat fresh fruits and vegetables soon after they bought them. As fruits and vegetables ripen, they release a gas that causes them to spoil. When they are kept cool, the spoiling process slows down. The invention of the refrigerator helped solve the problem of fruits and vegetables quickly spoiling. Today, new technologies are still being developed to keep food fresh. There are certain minerals that absorb the gas that causes fruit and vegetables to spoil. Special green food-storage bags are made with these minerals. Fruits and vegetables stored in these bags stay fresh even longer.

There are other technologies for heating food. You can have an entire meal ready in minutes using a microwave oven. Some new stoves use electromagnets instead of gas or electricity to produce heat. These new stoves are also more efficient. They use less energy than gas or electric stoves and can boil water in 90 seconds.

7. ◎ **Cause and Effect** How has the technology to keep food fresh affected how you eat?

..........................................................

..........................................................

Green food-storage bag technology solves the problem of food quickly spoiling.

computer

microwave oven

## Technology at School

Many schools have public address systems so that announcements can be made to the entire school. These systems are a form of technology. The announcer speaks into a microphone where the sound is changed into electricity. The electricity travels through wires to speakers throughout the school. The speakers turn the electricity back into sound and you hear the announcement.

Many teachers have started using electronic white boards to teach. These white boards allow the students to learn lessons in a different way. Students can interact with the white board.

public address system

**8. Infer** How do you think an electronic white board could be used in your classroom?

.................................................................

electronic white board

## Got it?

🕐 4.4.1, 4.DP.1

**9.** UNLOCK THE BIG Q     Identify one technology you use everyday. How does if affect your life?

.................................................................

.................................................................

**10. Explain** How has train transportation changed over time?

.................................................................

.................................................................

.................................................................

⏹ **Stop!** I need help with .................................................................

⏸ **Wait!** I have a question about .................................................................

▶ **Go!** Now I know .................................................................

## Lesson 2

# What is the design process?

4.4.1 Investigate transportation systems and devices that operate on or in land, water, air, and space and recognize the forces (lift, drag, friction, thrust and gravity) that affect their motion. 4.DP.4 Select a solution to the need or problem. (Also 4.DP.5, 4.DP.10)

## Envision It!

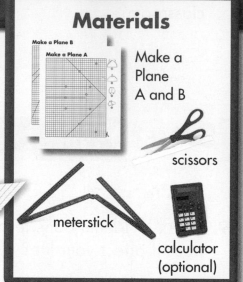

Why do you think these aircraft have different designs?

## Inquiry Explore It!

### How can the design of a model help you learn about the real thing?

☑ 1. Make 2 paper planes (**models**) with wings of different shapes but the same size (area). Plane A has wide, short wings. Plane B has long, narrow wings.

☑ 2. Make a plan to test how far each plane flies. Test each plane 3 times. **Record** your **data.**

### Materials

Make a Plane A and B

scissors

meterstick

calculator (optional)

### Explain Your Results

3. **Draw a Conclusion** How might the shape of a plane's wings affect how far it flies?

......................................

......................................

4. **Communicate** Based on what you learned, discuss the shape of wings on passenger planes.

#### Effect of Wing Shape on Distance Traveled

| Trial | Distance Traveled (meters) | |
|---|---|---|
| | Plane A (wide, short wings) | Plane B (long, narrow wings) |
| 1 | | |
| 2 | | |
| 3 | | |
| Average | | |

myscienceonline.com | **Explore It!** Animation

4.NS.5 Use measurement skills and apply appropriate units when collecting data. 4.DP.8 Evaluate and test the design using measurement. 4.DP.9 Present evidence using mathematical representations (graphs, data tables). (Also 4.4.4, 4.NS.7)

**Words to Know**

design process
prototype

## Design Process

People often have problems that can be solved with a new product or an improved process. For example, people have always looked for faster ways to travel from one place to another.

Orville and Wilbur Wright had a dream to design the world's first piloted-and-powered flying machine. Other inventors had created gliders. A glider is a kind of aircraft that can sail from a high place to a lower one without a motor. Early gliders were difficult to control. After many experiments, Orville and Wilbur invented a way to control flight. On December 17, 1903, their motorized airplane, the *Flyer,* flew for 12 seconds.

The way the Wright brothers designed the airplane can show how the design process is used. The **design process** is a set of steps for developing products and processes that solve problems.

1. **Underline** the definition of the design process.

2. **Predict** Why is it important to use the design process when developing a new product?

...............................................................

...............................................................

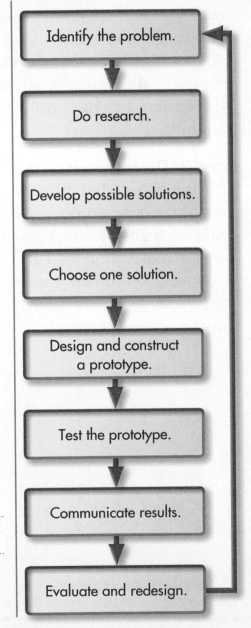

Identify the problem.

Do research.

Develop possible solutions.

Choose one solution.

Design and construct a prototype.

Test the prototype.

Communicate results.

Evaluate and redesign.

## Steps of the Design Process

Many people such as engineers and scientists use the design process when forming a solution to a problem. They may use different steps or use them in a different order. However, the goal to find a solution to a problem remains the same.

### Step 1: Identify the problem.

The first step in the design process is to identify the problem. One of the problems the Wright brothers noticed was that aircraft could not turn easily.

When you identify the problem, it is also important to identify who will benefit from your solution. If they could control how the airplane turned, then it could be used by almost anyone who wanted to learn how to fly. Modern passenger airplanes are designed to be used by highly-trained pilots, while other airplanes can be used by people with only a small amount of training. People who want to quickly travel long distances benefit from the airplane.

### Step 2: Do research.

Researching what others have learned is an important part of the design process. Orville and Wilbur researched what others had learned about flight. They talked to other inventors and read about the experiments of other inventors. You can do research by using the Internet, encyclopedias, informational books, and by interviewing experts on the subject.

3. **Identify** Name a problem that can be solved by a new design. Who would use your design?

..................................................

..................................................

..................................................

..................................................

..................................................

4. **Infer** Why do you think research is important?

..................................................

..................................................

..................................................

..................................................

The Wright brothers researched the work of Sir George Cayley. Here is one of Sir Cayley's diagrams.

This picture shows one of Otto Lilienthal's gliding experiments. His work was also part of the Wrights' research.

myscienceonline.com  THE BIG  I Will Know...

## Step 3: Develop possible solutions.

The next step is to think of one or more solutions to the problem. Wilbur decided to make airplane wings that could be twisted. The wings could then be moved to turn the plane. Orville and Wilbur called twisting the wings of the plane "wing-warping."

It is important to measure the size and weight and to identify the shape of each part of your design. How much each part weighs can affect how your design works. Drawing or building a model of your solution helps you determine which solution is best.

Math and science will help you develop possible solutions to your design problem. The Wright brothers made careful measurements and calculations to perfect the design of the airplane. Knowledge of scientific principles related to motion helped them develop solutions.

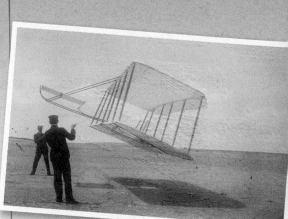

*Orville and Wilbur adjusted the wing shape of this kite to experiment with wing-warping.*

5. **Compare** Look at the captions and images on this page. How has adjusting an aircraft's wing shape changed?

......................................................................

......................................................................

......................................................................

The rudder and the elevator also help control the plane during turns.

— Rudder

— Elevator

— Aileron

Modern aircraft use ailerons instead of wing-warping to adjust the shape of the wings.

## Step 4: Choose one solution.

In the design process, several factors can influence the solution that you choose. The solution must solve the problem you identified. The solution must also be affordable. If your solution costs too much, you may not be able to sell it. The amount of time you have can also affect which solution you choose. Safety is another factor to consider when choosing a solution.

When choosing a solution, engineers have to make trade-offs. If a plane design is fast, but not safe, a safer design should be chosen. You should save all the plans you have for other possible solutions because you may need them in the future.

## Step 5: Design and construct a prototype.

Next, you need to carefully construct a prototype using the plans you have created for that solution. A **prototype** is the first fully working product that uses your design solution.

You should identify the materials and tools you need to construct your solution. Flexibility, strength, and hardness are three important properties you might consider when choosing materials. Different tools are also used for completing different tasks of the solution. The Wright brothers built several gliders and airplanes as they searched for solutions to the problem of controlling flight.

6. ◎ **Cause and Effect Underline** the factors that may affect which solution you choose to build.

7. **Explain** What materials do you think the Wright brothers used to construct the wings of their plane? Why?

........................................

........................................

........................................

........................................

........................................

........................................

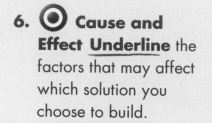

After building a prototype, this aeronautical engineer will test it in a wind tunnel.

## Step 6: Test the prototype.

The product needs to be carefully tested to see if it works safely and solves the problem it was designed for. Tests should use careful measurements. Recording the results of the tests you do will help you make adjustments to your design. After the tests, you should evaluate whether or not your product solved the problem.

Orville and Wilbur tested their gliders and planes. They observed how well the plane was controlled and made changes to their design to improve control during turns.

*The Wright brothers used this glider to test their ideas.*

**8. Infer** Why do you think it is important to record your measurements and observations?

........................................................................

........................................................................

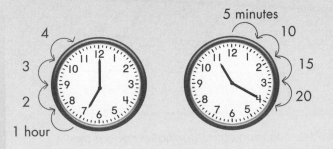

## Do the math!

### Elapsed Time

The Wrights measured the elapsed time from take-off to landing for each flight. Elapsed time is the amount of time that passes from the start time to the end time. A flight departs at 7:00 A.M. and arrives at 11:20 A.M. How long is the flight?
Find the starting time.
Count the hours.     Count the minutes.

4
3
2
1 hour

5 minutes
10
15
20

The flight lasted 4 hours, 20 minutes.

Find the elapsed time for each flight.

**1** Departure Time: 9:00 A.M.
Arrival Time: 10:45 A.M.

........................................................................

**2** Departure Time: 1:30 P.M.
Arrival Time: 3:55 P.M.

........................................................................

**3** Departure Time: 11:00 A.M.
Arrival Time: 2:15 P.M.

........................................................................

## Step 7: Communicate results.

Many times, a team of people work together to design a solution to a problem. It is important to document and communicate with your team members the solution, and the data, or evidence, you collect. There are many ways to document and communicate this information. Tables and graphs can help you communicate data. Labeled diagrams, graphic organizers, and lists are also helpful in communicating your solution to others. The procedure for building the solution and for the tests performed on it should be written carefully.

Other team members should be able to use your procedures, observations, and diagrams to do their own investigations. After you have communicated your results to others, they may help you find solutions to problems with your product.

Solving one problem may create new problems. You should think of ways your solution will affect society. The invention of the airplane made travel much quicker. This benefits the lives of many people. Some inventions can have harmful effects. Noise pollution is a common problem related to airplane technology.

9. **Identify** (Circle) two things you need to communicate to others about your product.

10. **Explain** Tell why diagrams can be an effective way to communicate information.

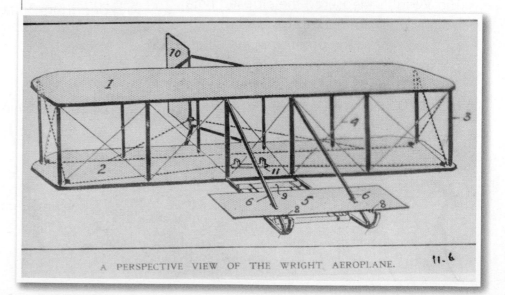

A PERSPECTIVE VIEW OF THE WRIGHT AEROPLANE.

11.6

*This diagram was used to communicate information about the design of the Wright brothers' invention to the U.S. Patent Office.*

## Step 8: Evaluate and redesign.

After testing your protoype, you should evaluate how well it solves the problem. You may need to redesign your product. Orville and Wilbur redesigned their airplane many times. Since then, airplanes have been redesigned many times by many other people. Modern airplanes have many different designs because they have different purposes. Planes travel faster and farther today than the planes the Wright brothers made.

Redesigning your product will help solve some of the problems that you discovered as you tested it. The new solution should go through the design process again.

*This modern jet solves the problem of turning in a different way.*

11. **Contrast** Explain one way this modern airplane is different from the Wright brother's first successful airplane.

..............................................................................

..............................................................................

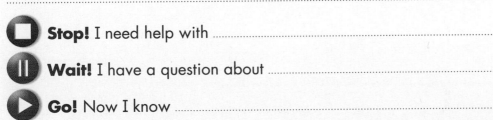

**Got it?**  🕐 4.4.1, 4.DP.4, 4.DP.5, 4.DP.10

12. **Identify** What are the steps in the design process?

..............................................................................

..............................................................................

..............................................................................

13. **Judge** Why do you think it is important to communicate your solution to others?

..............................................................................

..............................................................................

⬜ **Stop!** I need help with ....................................................

⏸ **Wait!** I have a question about ..........................................

▶ **Go!** Now I know ...........................................................

## Which boat design will hold more cargo?

### Follow a Procedure

☑ **1. Make a Model**
Make a boat out of clay.
Make a boat of the same size and shape out of foil.
Pennies are the cargo your boat will hold.

☑ **2.** Place each boat in water.
Record your **observations.**

☑ **3. Predict** which boat will hold more pennies.
Record your prediction.

☑ **4.** Dry off the clay boat. Place it back in the water.
Place a penny in the boat.
Keep adding pennies until the boat sinks.
**Record** your **data.**

☑ **5.** Repeat Step 4 with the foil boat.

## Materials

clay

pennies

heavy-duty
aluminum foil

plastic tub of water

### Inquiry Skill
**Making a model** can help you make inferences about objects and events that are too large to test.

*Be sure your boats are the same size and shape.*

**4.DP.10** Communicate the solution including evidence using mathematical representations (graphs, data tables), drawings or prototypes.
**4.NS.9** Compare the results of an investigation with the prediction. (Also **4.DP.9, 4.4.1, 4.4.4**)

| Observations of Boats With and Without Cargo | | |
|---|---|---|
| **Boat** | **Without Cargo** | **With Cargo** |
| Clay | | |
| Foil | | |

## Analyze and Conclude

**6.** Which boat floated better without cargo?

.................................................................................................

.................................................................................................

**7.** How many pennies did each boat hold?
Did your **observations** support your **predictions**?

.................................................................................................

.................................................................................................

**8. Infer** Compare your boat **design** with those of other groups.
What inferences can you make about boat design based on this activity?

.................................................................................................

.................................................................................................

**9.** UNLOCK THE BIG Q   How can physical models help engineers design
boats and ships?

.................................................................................................

.................................................................................................

.................................................................................................

🖊 4.DP.1

# Robotics Engineer

Have you ever wanted to build a machine to make a chore simpler? Have you wanted to create special effects for movies or theme parks? You may be interested in a career as a robotics engineer!

Robotics engineers are also called roboticists. They design and build machines to perform tasks. Designing robots takes a wide combination of skills and knowledge. For example, once roboticists identify the task a robot will perform, they must test different kinds of materials to see what the robot will be made of. They must also decide on the robot's power source. Finally, roboticists must program the robot to perform the task.

Because designing robots involves so many branches of science, roboticists often work in teams, with each person focusing on one or two areas of the job. Robotics engineers often study electrical engineering, mechanical engineering, and computer science.

Why might a robotics engineer need to study both mechanical and electrical engineering?

# Vocabulary Smart Cards

technology
design process
prototype

## Play a Game!

Cut out the Vocabulary Smart Cards.

Work with a partner. Choose a Vocabulary Smart Card. Do not let your partner see your card.

Draw a picture to show what the term means. Have your partner guess the term. Take turns drawing and guessing.

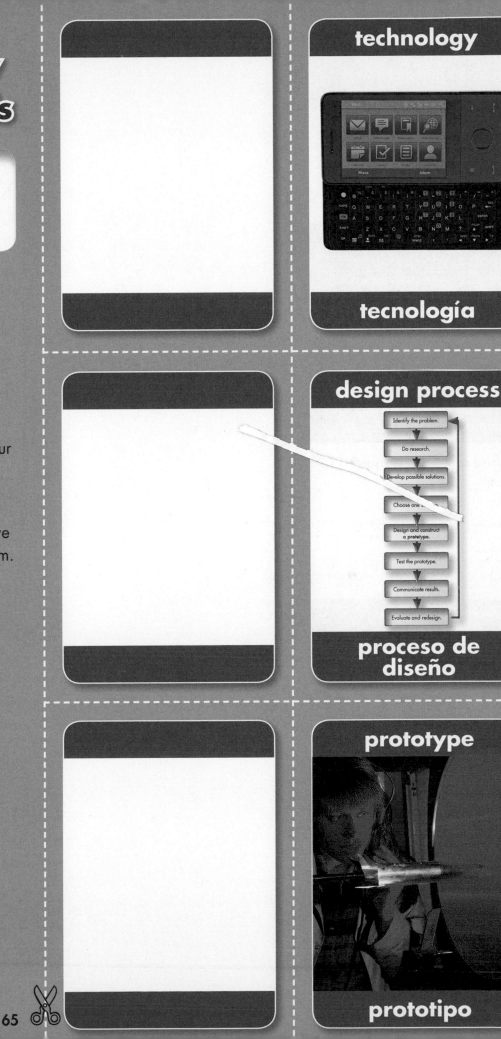

**technology**

tecnología

**design process**

Identify the problem.

Do research.

Develop possible solutions.

Choose one solution.

Design and construct a prototype.

Test the prototype.

Communicate results.

Evaluate and redesign.

proceso de diseño

**prototype**

prototipo

65

the knowledge, processes, and products that solve problems and make work easier

Write two examples.

......................................................

......................................................

el conocimiento, los procesos y los productos con que se resuelven los problemas y se facilita el trabajo

a set of steps for developing products and processes that solve problems

Write a sentence using this term.

......................................................

......................................................

serie de pasos para desarrollar productos y procesos que resuelven problemas

first fully working product that uses a design solution

What is the prefix in this word and what does it mean?

......................................................

......................................................

el primer producto que demuestra una solución de diseño

# Interactive Vocabulary

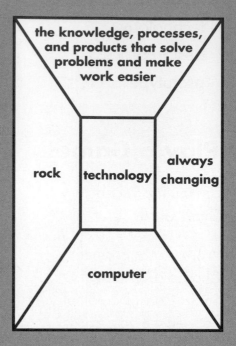

the knowledge, processes, and products that solve problems and make work easier

rock | technology | always changing

computer

## Make a Word Square!

Choose a vocabulary term and write it in the center of the square. Fill in the other spaces with a definition, a characteristic, an example, and something that is not an example.

## Lesson 1

### What is technology?

- Technology can help solve problems and make work easier.
- Transportation technologies help move people and products quickly and safely from place to place.

## Lesson 2

### What is the design process?

- The design process is a set of steps for developing products and processes that solve problems.
- A prototype is the first fully working product that uses your solution.

# Chapter Review

 How does technology affect our lives?

## Lesson 1    4.4.1

**What is technology?**

**1. Infer** Why is technology important?

..............................................................

..............................................................

..............................................................

..............................................................

..............................................................

..............................................................

**2. Write About It** Explain how trains have changed over time.

..............................................................

..............................................................

..............................................................

..............................................................

..............................................................

..............................................................

..............................................................

**3.** **Do the math!** Suppose a car travels 70 kilometers per hour. How far will the car travel in 3 hours and 30 minutes?

..............................................................

..............................................................

**4. Predict** How do you think a magnetic levitation train would affect your community?

..............................................................

..............................................................

..............................................................

..............................................................

..............................................................

..............................................................

**5.** **Cause and Effect** Explain how technology affects your school.

..............................................................

..............................................................

..............................................................

..............................................................

..............................................................

..............................................................

**Lesson 2**  🔲 4.4.1, 4.DP.4, 4.DP.5, 4.DP.10

**What is the design process?**

6. **Vocabulary** Which of the following is
   NOT a step in the design process?
   A. Do research.
   B. Construct a prototype.
   C. Identify and control variables.
   D. Redesign.

7. **Explain** How might cost affect which
   prototype you choose to build?

   .................................................

   .................................................

   .................................................

   .................................................

   .................................................

   .................................................

8. **Infer** Why do you think engineers build
   prototypes of their designs?

   .................................................

   .................................................

   .................................................

   .................................................

9. **Identify** What are two steps in the
   design process that the Wright brothers
   used when building their plane?

   .................................................

   .................................................

   .................................................

   .................................................

   .................................................

   .................................................

   .................................................

   .................................................

10. **APPLY THE BIG** How does technology affect
    our lives?

    ....................................................

    Choose a transportation technology
    and explain how it affects your life.

    .................................................

    .................................................

    .................................................

    .................................................

    .................................................

    .................................................

## Multiple Choice

**1** A prototype is ............................................

    A. a procedure for building a solution.

    B. the first fully working product that uses your design solution.

    C. a final solution.

    D. a set of steps that solve problems.

 **4.DP.1**

## Constructed Response

**2** Explain how an engineer might use the design process to build a bridge.

....................................................................................

....................................................................................

....................................................................................

....................................................................................

....................................................................................

....................................................................................

....................................................................................

....................................................................................

....................................................................................

....................................................................................

....................................................................................

 **4.4.4**

## Extended Response

**3** A toy maker wants to see how mass affects the speed of a toy car. The cars are used on a downhill track. He tests five cars. Each car has a different mass, but has the same size and shape.

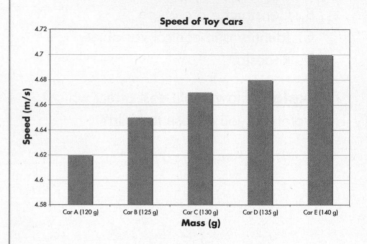

What does the graph show about how mass affects the speed of a toy car in this experiment?

....................................................................................

....................................................................................

How could the toy maker use this information to design a faster car?

....................................................................................

....................................................................................

What else do you think might affect how fast the toy car moves?

....................................................................................

....................................................................................

 **4.4.4**

# Green Transportation

One of the biggest problems with transportation today is air pollution. Cars, trains, planes, and ships all release pollutants. Many transportation technologies release carbon dioxide. Carbon dioxide is a pollutant that contributes to global climate change.

You may wonder how you can reduce air pollution. There are many ways. You can choose to walk to a friend's house instead of getting a ride. If you need to go a longer distance you can ride a bike, take a bus, or ride on a train. Some people travel in carpools. A carpool is when two or more people meet to travel together. Using a bus, train, or carpool helps to reduce the number of cars on the road. Fewer cars mean less pollution.

Some technologies help to reduce the amount of pollution cars produce. Hybrid cars can run on electricity and gasoline. This reduces the amount of pollution they produce. Cars today have catalytic converters. This technology changes some of the toxic gases given off by an engine to less harmful gases.

**APPLY THE BIG Q**

What is a positive effect of transportation technology?

...................................................................................................................

...................................................................................................................

What is a negative effect of transportation technology?

...................................................................................................................

...................................................................................................................

# What affects motion?

# Technology and Motion

**Try It!** How can you measure motion?

**Lesson 1** What is motion?

**Lesson 2** What is speed?
4.4.2

**Lesson 3** How do forces affect motion?
4.4.1, 4.4.3

**Investigate It!** How can friction affect motion?

These cyclists are riding on a circular racing track. This track has curves and banks so that the cyclists can move very quickly.

**Predict** What might affect the cyclists' motion?

.........................................................................................

.........................................................................................

.........................................................................................

How can motion be described and measured?

## How can you measure motion?

Motion is a change in the position of an object. In this activity you determine a way to measure motion.

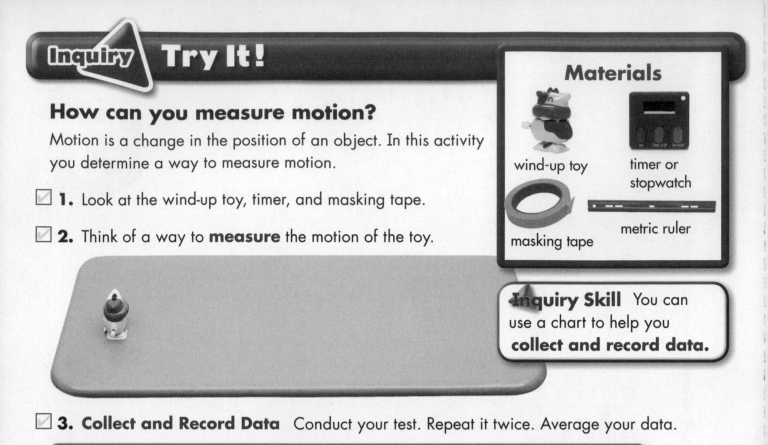

### Materials

wind-up toy

timer or stopwatch

masking tape

metric ruler

☑ **1.** Look at the wind-up toy, timer, and masking tape.

☑ **2.** Think of a way to **measure** the motion of the toy.

> **Inquiry Skill** You can use a chart to help you **collect and record data.**

☑ **3. Collect and Record Data** Conduct your test. Repeat it twice. Average your data.

| Data Table | | | |
|---|---|---|---|
| **Trial** | | | |
| 1 | | | |
| 2 | | | |
| 3 | | | |
| **Average** | | | |

## Explain Your Results

**4.**  **Interpret Data** Was your data the same each time? ............................. Explain why your data may have varied. Compare your data with the data of other groups.

...............................................................................................................

...............................................................................................................

...............................................................................................................

**5.** How did you **measure** motion?

...............................................................................................................

...............................................................................................................

**4.4.2** Make appropriate measurements to compare the speeds of objects in terms of distance traveled in a given amount of time or time required to travel a given distance. (Also **4.NS.5**)

## ◉ Sequence

- Sequence refers to the order in which events happen.
- Words such as *first, next, then, after,* and *finally* signal sequence.

### Ramp and Marble

First, my friend gave me a ruler with a groove in the center. Next, I put one end of the ruler on the floor. Then, I propped the other end on a book to form a ramp. Finally, I put a marble in the groove at the high end of the ruler and let it go.

## Practice It!

Circle clue words in the above reading. Then complete the graphic organizer to show the sequence in which things happened.

**First**

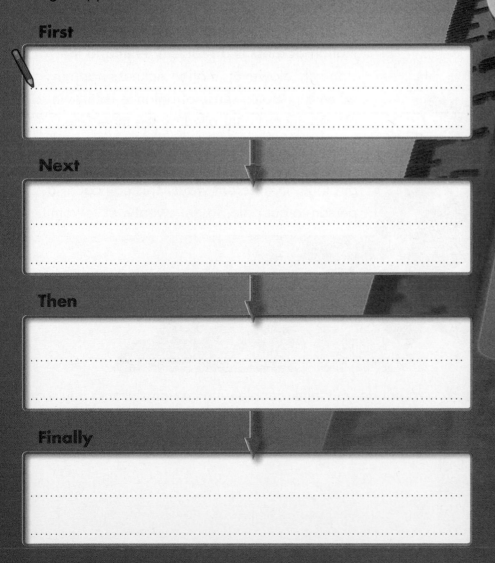

**Next**

**Then**

**Finally**

# Lesson 1
## What is motion?

**Envision It!**

Draw the path that the bouncing ball takes.

## my planet diary

### //// MISCONCEPTION ////

Have you ever felt sick in a car, a boat, a train, or an airplane? You may have had motion sickness. Some people think that motion sickness is a problem related to the stomach. However, motion sickness happens when a person's sense of balance is thrown off. Balance is controlled by the inner ear. Sometimes the inner ear and the eyes process riding in something, such as a car or an airplane, in different ways. This can cause a person to get pale, to get sweaty, or to vomit.

What do you think people with motion sickness could do to feel better?

........................................................

........................................................

........................................................

I will know that objects move in different ways. I will know how to use a reference point.

**Words to Know**

motion
reference point

## Motion

All kinds of things around you move in different ways. Objects can move in a straight line, in a curved path, back and forth as a vibration, or as a rotation. You can describe and measure their motion in different ways. **Motion** is a change in the position of an object.

Look at the toy car and track in the picture to the right. First, the car moves in a straight path. Next, the car moves in curves around the track. Finally, the car moves back to the starting line.

Sometimes toy cars move in a curved path on the track.

Sometimes the cars move in a straight path.

1. ◎ **Sequence** Describe the sequence of events of the yellow race car as it travels around the track.

2. **Identify** Which types of motion are not present in this image?

........................................

........................................

........................................

**First**

[ ............................................................ ]

**Next**

[ ............................................................ ]

**Finally**

[ ............................................................ ]

## Relative Motion

How do you know if a person on a water slide moves? How do you know if the water moves? You look at the changing positions of the person and the water. You compare the person's changing positions with the fixed position of the slide. You use the motion of the objects around you to decide what is moving and what is not moving. Since the slide does not seem to be moving relative to you, it must be the person and the water that are moving.

Every day, you compare objects that change position with objects that do not. The change in one object's position compared with another object's position is called relative motion. For example, suppose that you and your friend are sitting in a school bus. The bus begins to move. To you, your friend does not appear to move, but the people outside the bus appear to be moving. To the people watching the bus, you and your friend are moving.

As you ride your bicycle or walk down a street, you may pass trees or street lamps. At first you see them far ahead of you, moving toward you. Eventually you see them pass you by. If you turn your head to look back, you can see them moving away from you. Are they moving, or are you moving?

3. ◎ **Sequence**
**Underline** the steps you take to tell if a person on a water slide moves. Then number each step.

4. **Locate Draw** an ✗ on a reference point for the people in the tube. **Circle** a moving object.

You would normally say that you are moving forward relative to the trees and street lamps. However, you could also say that they are moving backward relative to you! Just as the position of the trees and street lamps changes compared to yours, your position also changes compared to theirs. This can be confusing, so when an object and the ground change position relative to each other, we usually say that the object is moving and the ground is not.

5. **CHALLENGE** Besides using a reference point, what is another way to determine if you are moving?

....................................................................

....................................................................

*When you enter a loop on the water slide, you are moving in many ways. You are sliding, twisting, turning, and moving faster.*

*When you finish moving down the slide, you enter a pool of water. Sometimes it is difficult to determine your motion or location because you have to find a reference point.*

## At-Home Lab

### Mark Your Point
List three things that do not seem to move relative to you as you ride or walk home from school. List three things that do seem to move relative to you. Which objects help you determine that you are moving?

## Reference Points

A **reference point** is a place or object used to determine if an object is in motion. When you ride in a car, you can tell your car is moving by observing a sign or a building. They appear to come and go. Many objects can be reference points.

Objects that do not seem to move define your frame of reference. Your frame of reference is like your point of view. How an object seems to move depends on your frame of reference.

In the picture above, the three people are passing many trees. They also may have different motions compared to each other, because they may not be riding at the same speed.

6. **Infer** If the bikers move at the same speed and the biker in the back uses only the biker in front as a reference, what might the biker in the back conclude about his or her own motion?

........................................................................................

........................................................................................

When you stop for a break during a long bicycle ride, have you really stopped moving? You are probably using the ground as your reference point. Since your position is not changing relative to the ground, you would say that you are not moving. But suppose you use the sun as your reference point instead. Earth is moving around the sun at great speed, and you are moving along with Earth! Motion depends on your reference point.

## Got it?

**8. Define** What is motion and why is it relative?

...........................................................................................................

...........................................................................................................

...........................................................................................................

**9. Support** How do you know if you are moving when you are riding on a train?

...........................................................................................................

...........................................................................................................

⬛ **Stop!** I need help with ................................................................

⏸ **Wait!** I have a question about ....................................................

▶ **Go!** Now I know ..........................................................................

# Lesson 2
# What is speed?

**4.4.2** Make appropriate measurements to compare the speeds of objects in terms of distance traveled in a given amount of time or time required to travel a given distance.

Which animal do you think would win a 100-meter race?

## Inquiry Explore It!

### What can change a marble's speed?

**Materials**

2 books

masking tape

metal marble

ruler

calculator or computer (optional)

meterstick

timer

☑ **1.** Roll a marble down a ramp. Time how long it takes the marble to move 180 cm.
.............. sec
Find the speed.
.............. cm/sec

speed = distance ÷ time

*Place marble at end of ruler.*

start

*Use tape to label the start and the finish.*

☑ **2. Predict** how raising the ramp would change the speed.

..........................................................................

Test your prediction by adding 1 book.
Time to move 180 cm = .............. sec
Speed = .............. cm/sec

### Explain Your Results

**3. Draw a Conclusion**  How did raising the ramp change the marble's speed?

..........................................................................

myscienceonline.com | ▶ xplore It! Animation

**4.4.3** investigate how changes in speed or direction are caused by forces; the greater the force exerted on an object, the greater the change. (Also **4.NS.1, 4.NS.5, 4.NS.9**)

**Rank the animals from highest speed to lowest speed. Put a 1, 2, or 3 in the box next to each animal.**

**Words to Know**

speed
velocity

# Speed

Objects move at different speeds. **Speed** is the rate at which an object changes position. Speed measures how fast an object moves. The unit for speed is a unit of distance divided by a unit of time, such as kilometers per hour. A car moving at a high speed changes position faster than a car moving at a slow speed.

Many animals run faster than humans. The fastest land mammal is the cheetah. It can run at speeds around 70 miles per hour or 112 kilometers per hour. A peregrine falcon is also very fast. When it swoops to capture prey, the falcon moves at almost 275 miles per hour! In the pictures above, which animals do you think are faster than you?

1. **Locate** (Circle) the main idea. Underline the details.

2. **Compute** How much faster is the top speed of a peregrine falcon than that of the cheetah?

...............................................................

3. **Describe** How could you describe the speed of this rowboat?

...............................

...............................

...............................

...............................

## Calculate Average Speed

The speed of most objects changes. For example, when you ride your bike, you do not always travel at the same speed. At different points on your trip, you will have different speeds. However, you can calculate the average speed of your trip. To find an object's average speed, divide the distance the object moves by the total time spent moving.

To calculate average speed, you use this equation:

$$\text{Average Speed} = \frac{\text{total distance}}{\text{total time}}$$

Look at the map on these pages. The map shows the route a car traveled from point A to point D.

**Point A**

**Point B**

The car traveled from point A to point B in 2 hours (hr). The distance from point A to point B is 120 kilometers (km). To calculate the car's average speed for this trip, divide 120 km by 2 hr.

$$\text{Average Speed} = \frac{120 \text{ km}}{2 \text{ hr}}$$

$$\text{Average Speed} = \frac{60 \text{ km}}{1 \text{ hr}}$$

$$\text{Average Speed} = 60 \frac{\text{km}}{\text{hr}}$$

So the car traveled at an average speed of 60 kilometers per hour from point A to point B.

## At-Home Lab

**On a Roll**

Work in an open area. Mark a starting point. Roll a ball from the starting point. Mark where the ball stopped. Roll the ball from the starting point again. Use more force. Make a statement about the speed of the ball. Base your statements on your observations.

20 mi

20 km

myscienceonline.com | THE BIG | I Will Know...

The car traveled 231 kilometers from point B to point C in 3 hours.

$$\text{Speed} = \frac{231 \text{ km}}{3 \text{ hr}}$$

**4. Calculate** What was the average speed for this leg of the trip? Show your work.

The car traveled 90 kilometers from point C to point D in 2 hours.

**5. Calculate** What was the average speed for this leg of the trip? Show your work.

**Point D**

**Point C**

**6. CHALLENGE** What was the average speed for the entire trip from point A to point D? Show your work.

# Velocity and Acceleration

Some objects change speed *and direction*. **Velocity** is both the speed and the direction an object is moving. Some words that describe direction are *north, south, east,* and *west*. Others are *left, right, up,* and *down*.

Any change in the speed or direction of an object's motion is acceleration. Starting, speeding up, and slowing down are accelerations. The roller coaster accelerates as it speeds up or slows down. It is changing speed. A roller coaster on a curved path accelerates even if its speed does not change. That is because it changes direction as it moves around the curve.

7. **Decide** Which of the following is NOT an example of an acceleration?
   a. An airplane moving at the same speed in the same direction
   b. An airplane slowing its speed and moving down to land
   c. An airplane slowing its speed and moving in the same direction

8. **Summarize** What are two things that must be measured in order to find an object's velocity?

9. **Illustrate** Look at the roller coaster on the opposite page. Draw a solid arrow where the roller coaster slows down, and a dotted arrow where the coaster speeds up.

## Do the math!

### Calculate Percentages

Race cars travel quickly around racetracks. To determine how much of the track has been traveled, fill in the chart by finding the fraction, decimal, and percentage. The first row is done for you.

| Amount of Track Traveled | | |
|---|---|---|
| Fraction | Decimal | Percentage |
| $\frac{80}{100}$ | 0.80 | 80% |
| $\frac{50}{100}$ | 0.50 | |
| $\frac{35}{100}$ | | |
| | 0.25 | 25% |

myscienceonline.com | Got it? 60-Second Video

........................................

........................................

........................................

........................................

........................................

**Got it?** ⏱ 4.4.2

11. **Produce** How do you calculate average speed?

........................................

........................................

12.  **Distinguish** What is the difference between speed and velocity?

........................................

........................................

........................................

........................................

■ **Stop!** I need help with ........................................

❚❚ **Wait!** I have a question about ........................................

▶ **Go!** Now I know ........................................

# Lesson 3

## How do forces affect motion?

4.4.1 Investigate transportation systems and devices that operate on or in land, water, air and space and recognize the forces (lift, drag, friction, thrust and gravity) that affect their motion. (Also 4.4.3)

### Envision It!

Tell how you think this train moves.

## Inquiry Explore It!

### How can forces move paper?

☑ **1.** Use a strip of paper. Tape the edges together to make a loop. Hang the loop on a pencil.

☑ **2.** **Predict** what will happen to the paper if you blow across its top.

.................................................

.................................................

☑ **3.** Blow across the top of the paper. **Record** your **observations.** Draw arrows on the picture to show how the paper moved.

### Explain Your Results

**4.** **Infer** Forces act upon objects to move them. In what direction did forces act on the paper?

.................................................

.................................................

.................................................

### Materials

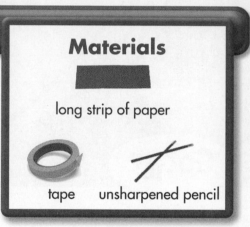

long strip of paper

tape    unsharpened pencil

myscienceonline.com | Explore It! Animation

4.4.3 investigate how changes in speed or direction are caused by forces; the greater the force exerted on an object, the greater the change. (Also 4.NS.1)

I will know what affects the motion of objects.

## Words to Know

| | |
|---|---|
| force | thrust |
| friction | drag |
| lift | gravity |

## Forces and Motion

Objects do not just start to move on their own. For example, a marble on a level surface will not move unless you hit it with your finger or another object. Something must make the marble start to roll. Something must also make a rolling marble stop. The thing that does this is called a force. A **force** is any push or pull.

If an object is standing still, it will only move if a force acts on it. Then, the object starts to move in the direction of the force. If the object is already moving, a force can make it move faster, slow down, change direction, or stop. In other words, a moving object will keep the same speed and direction as long as no force is acting on it. An object at rest will stay at rest unless a force acts on it.

1. **Locate Underline** in the second paragraph the five ways a force can affect motion.

2. **Explain** What do you think the force does to the blue marble? What does the force do to the yellow marble?

.......................................................................

.......................................................................

.......................................................................

.......................................................................

*A moving marble hits a blue marble that is standing still.*

## Contact and Non-Contact Forces

Some forces act only on contact. A contact force must touch an object to affect it. For example, a marble on a level surface will not move until you hit it with your finger or with another object. Contact starts the marble rolling. You exert contact forces when you pull something with a rope or when you kick a football.

Other forces can act at a distance. These forces can affect objects without touching them. These forces are called non-contact forces. An example of a non-contact force is magnetism. Without any contact, a magnet can pull iron marbles. The magnet has a force that acts on the iron from a distance.

Pushing or pulling can change both the position and motion of an object. The size of the change depends on the strength of the push or pull. For example, the harder you push a swing, the higher and faster it will move.

**3. Locate Underline** in the second paragraph the explanation of what a non-contact force is.

**4. Explain** Six iron marbles are placed between two magnets What do you think will happen if the marbles are not touching the magnets?

..................................................

..................................................

..................................................

..................................................

..................................................

..................................................

## Combined Forces

All forces have both size and direction. Two forces acting in opposite directions can balance each other out. Notice the dogs pulling on the rubber toy. They are combining forces, but they are working against each other. They are pulling in opposite directions with the same amount of force. As long as they both pull equally hard, the forces are balanced. Neither force will change the motion of the toy. If one dog pulls with more force, the forces will be unbalanced. The toy will move toward the dog pulling with a greater force.

Combined forces can work together as well. Suppose you are asked to move a heavy table across a room. You might have trouble doing it yourself, but the job becomes easier with a friend's help. If you both push or pull in the same direction, you will be combining your forces. When two forces act on the same object and in the same direction, they add up to a bigger force. A bigger force will cause a bigger change in the motion of the object.

*Some trains are pulled by one engine from the front and pushed by a second engine from the back. The total force combines the forces of the engines.*

5. **Decide** What will happen if the black-and-white puppy lets go of the toy? Draw arrows to show what might happen.

.................................................

.................................................

.................................................

.................................................

.................................................

# Friction

Objects in motion are slowed down by a force called friction. **Friction** is a force that acts when two surfaces rub together. It can slow or stop moving objects. You see friction in action when you give a box a push and it moves across the floor. Eventually, friction slows down the box and causes it to stop. Friction can even keep objects from starting to move at all. For example, it can keep dead leaves from sliding down a slanted roof.

Smoothness is one of several factors that can affect friction. Smooth surfaces often produce less friction than rough surfaces. Air and water can also produce some friction. Objects moving in outer space are free from friction.

# Land Transportation

There is always a need to carry people and things to work, to school, and to other cities. Transportation systems designed for land travel include cars, buses, and trains.

All land transportation systems must have a force that pushes or pulls them forward. For example, a car gets that force from an engine. To reduce friction with the ground, most land vehicles roll on wheels. Fast vehicles have streamlined shapes that reduce the friction of the air.

*The rider applies a force to the bike pedals. The pedals transfer this force to the chain and then to the rear wheel.*

*The brakes produce friction, a force that slows or stops the bike when necessary.*

6. **Apply** What would happen to the person sliding into the base if there were no friction?

7. **Contrast** The old-fashioned cable cars still used in some cities are pulled by cables. Name one advantage this system might have compared to a car.

myscienceonline.com | I Will Know...

## Water Transportation

Lakes, rivers, and the ocean provide great opportunities for transportation. We use boats, ships, and submarines to travel to distant places and to carry all kinds of goods.

Water offers some advantages and disadvantages for transportation. One disadvantage of water is that it makes it difficult to move very fast.

One advantage is that water can support heavy objects. An object immersed in water will be pushed up by the water with a force called buoyancy. If the weight of the object is less than the buoyant force acting on it, the object will float. The buoyant force of water can support the weight of large cargo ships weighing hundreds of tons!

To get back to the surface, a submarine pumps water out. This reduces the weight of the submarine.

The force of buoyancy depends only on the volume of the object. If you can make an object heavier or lighter without changing its volume, you can control whether it sinks or floats. A submarine goes underwater by filling special chambers with water and increasing its weight. When it empties those chambers, the submarine weighs less and rises to the surface.

## At-Home Lab

**Does it float?**
Fill a bucket or a plastic jug with tap water. Place an orange in the water. Does it float? Now peel the orange. Place the peeled orange in the water. Does it float? Explain your answers.

8. **Justify** How large do you think the buoyant force is on the ship below, compared to the weight of the ship? Explain

......................................................

......................................................

......................................................

......................................................

......................................................

## Air Transportation

Airplanes provide very fast transportation. This is useful when traveling long distances. For an airplane to stay in the air and to keep its velocity, four forces acting on the plane must be balanced.

When an airplane moves forward, air flows very fast over and under the wings. It pushes down from above and up from below, but the shape of the wings causes the push from below to be harder. The pushing force from below is called **lift.** At a certain speed, lift overcomes gravity and the plane can stay in the air.

The force that pushes or pulls the airplane forward is called **thrust.** When thrust and drag are balanced, the airplane keeps a constant speed.

**Drag** is a force caused by the air as the plane moves through it. The faster a plane goes, the stronger the drag becomes. Drag tends to slow down the airplane.

**Gravity** is the force that pulls all objects toward each other. Earth's gravity constantly pulls the airplane down. A heavy airplane is pulled down with more force than a light plane.

This person lets go of an apple. Earth's gravity pulls the apple toward Earth.

9. **Show** Draw arrows showing parts of the plane where you think the force of drag is pushing hard.

10. **Identify** Only two of the four forces listed above act on a falling skydiver. List the two forces.

myscienceonline.com | Got it? 60-Second Video

## Transportation in Space

How can the International Space Station stay in orbit year after year with its engines turned off? Remember that an object in motion will keep the same speed and direction if no forces act on it. In space there is no air or water to produce drag. A fast-moving spacecraft will not slow down if it turns off its engines. It will keep moving.

A spacecraft in orbit around Earth is pulled down by the force of gravity. Gravity changes the direction of motion of the spacecraft: instead of keeping a straight path, it moves in a curve around our planet.

**11. Show** Draw arrows to show the forces acting on the space station. How many forces are there?

......................................................................................

......................................................................................

......................................................................................

Motion in space is not slowed down by drag, but its direction can be changed by gravity.

## Got it?

⏸ 4.4.1

**12. Identify** What are some other land, water, air, and space transportation systems?

......................................................................................

......................................................................................

......................................................................................

**13. Design** Suppose you were asked to design stairs. What type of material would be good to use? Explain.

......................................................................................

......................................................................................

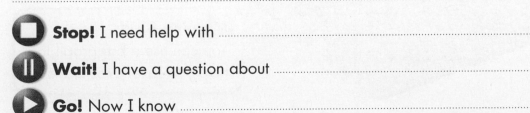

⏹ **Stop!** I need help with ....................................................

⏸ **Wait!** I have a question about ..........................................

▶ **Go!** Now I know ......................................................................

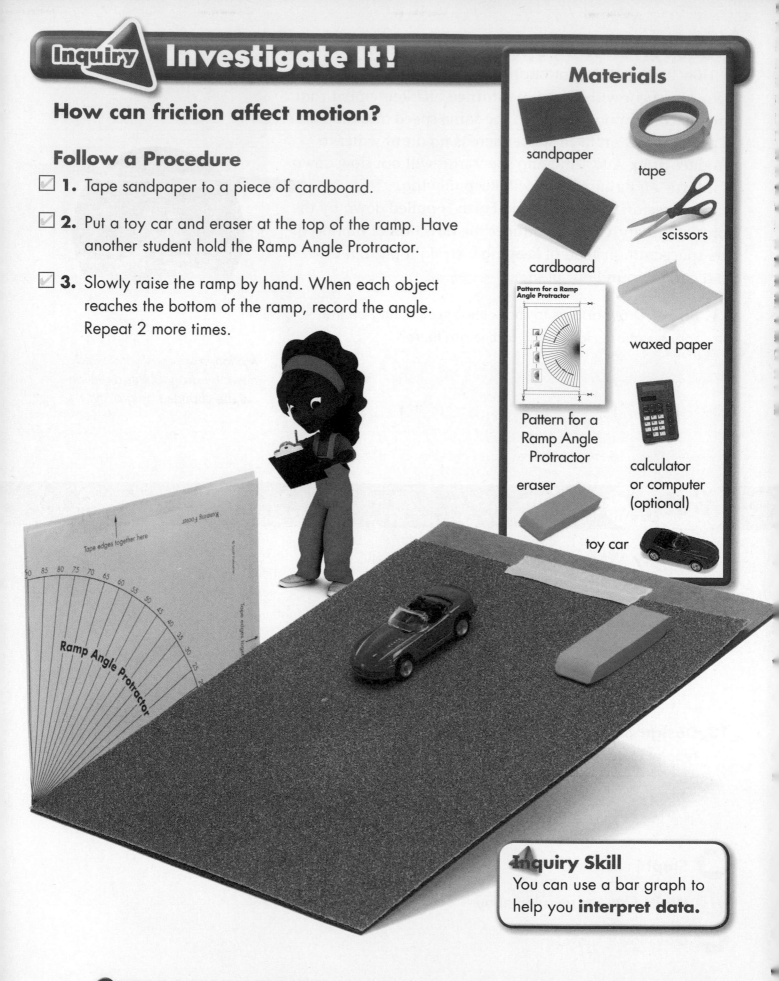

# Inquiry Investigate It!

## How can friction affect motion?

### Follow a Procedure

☑ **1.** Tape sandpaper to a piece of cardboard.

☑ **2.** Put a toy car and eraser at the top of the ramp. Have another student hold the Ramp Angle Protractor.

☑ **3.** Slowly raise the ramp by hand. When each object reaches the bottom of the ramp, record the angle. Repeat 2 more times.

## Materials

sandpaper

tape

scissors

cardboard

**Pattern for a Ramp Angle Protractor**

Pattern for a Ramp Angle Protractor

waxed paper

calculator or computer (optional)

eraser

toy car

Ramp Angle Protractor

Tape edges together here

Running Footer

### Inquiry Skill

You can use a bar graph to help you **interpret data.**

**4.4.1** Investigate transportation systems and devices that operate on or in land, water, air and space and recognize the forces (lift, drag, friction, thrust and gravity) that affect their motion. **4.4.3** Investigate how changes in speed or direction are caused by forces; the greater the force exerted on an object, the greater the change. **4.NS.6** Test predictions with multiple trials. (Also **4.NS.7, 4.DP.9**)

☑ **4. Predict** what would happen if you used waxed paper instead of sandpaper. Test your prediction 3 times. **Record** your results.

| Trial | Angle When Object Reached Bottom of Ramp (degrees) | | | |
|---|---|---|---|---|
| | **Sandpaper Surface** | | **Waxed-Paper Surface** | |
| | **Car** | **Eraser** | **Car** | **Eraser** |
| 1 | | | | |
| 2 | | | | |
| 3 | | | | |
| Average | | | | |

**Effect of Friction on Motion**

☑ **5.** Find the average angles. Make a bar graph of your results.

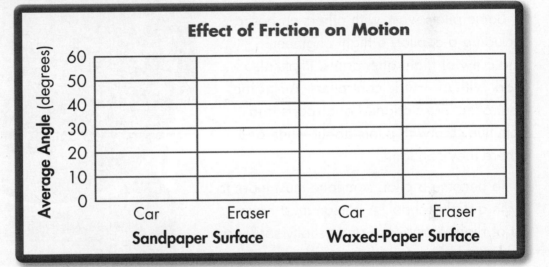

**Effect of Friction on Motion**

## Analyze and Conclude

**6. Interpret Data** How did changing surfaces affect the angle you recorded?

....................................................................................................

**7.** Describe how friction affected the motion of the objects on each surface.

....................................................................................................

....................................................................................................

....................................................................................................

# Science Careers

# Airline Pilot

4.4.1

An airplane pilot's job is to fly the plane safely. Pilots steer the plane and control its motion and velocity. A pilot uses the plane's engines to generate force to create motion. When the airplane is moving fast, the shape of its wings changes the air pressure around the plane and causes it to rise. The wings also can cause the plane to descend.

Some pilots work with others on board including a copilot, a flight engineer, and crew of flight attendants. Pilots also work with air traffic controllers. Air traffic controllers are stationed at airports and communicate with pilots about when and where they can land.

To become a pilot, someone must learn to fly in a flight school. A person must have a lot of flight experience and usually serves as a copilot before becoming a pilot.

APPLY THE BIG Q

Why do you think that pilots study motion and forces?

..................................................................

..................................................................

..................................................................

..................................................................

..................................................................

98

# Vocabulary Smart Cards

motion
reference point
speed
velocity
force
friction
lift
drag
thrust
gravity

## Vocabulary Sentences!

Cut out the Vocabulary Smart Cards.

Work with a partner. Choose a Vocabulary Smart Card. Write several sentences using the vocabulary word. Have your partner repeat using a different Vocabulary Smart Card.

velocity
velocidad

motion
movimiento

force
fuerza

reference point
punto de referencia

friction
fricción

speed
rapidez

a change in the position of an object

Write an example.

........................................................

........................................................

........................................................

........................................................

cambio en la posición de un objeto

---

the speed and the direction an object is moving

Write a sentence using this word.

........................................................

........................................................

........................................................

rapidez y dirección en que se mueve un objeto

---

# Interactive Vocabulary

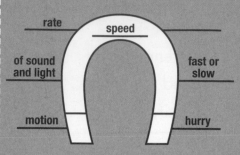

rate speed
of sound and light
fast or slow
motion hurry

## Make a Word Magnet

Choose a vocabulary word and write it in the Word Magnet. Write words that are related to it on the lines.

---

a place or object used to determine if an object is in motion

Draw an example.

lugar u objeto usado para determinar si algo está en movimiento

---

any push or pull

Draw an example.

empujón o jalón

---

the rate at which an object changes position

Write a sentence using this word.

........................................................

........................................................

........................................................

ritmo al cual cambia la posición de un objeto

---

a force that acts when two surfaces rub together

Draw an example.

fuerza que actúa cuando dos superficies se rozan

100

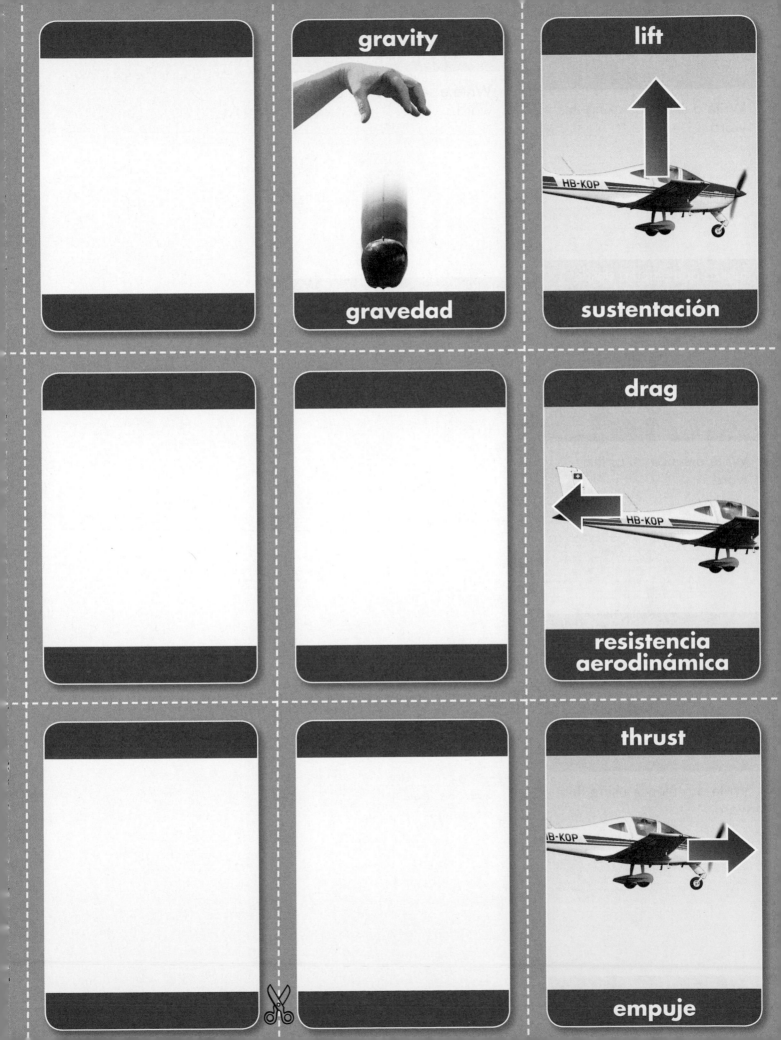

gravity

gravedad

lift

sustentación

drag

resistencia aerodinámica

thrust

empuje

## Card 1

a pushing force from below that keeps an airplane in the air

Write a sentence using this word.

........................................

........................................

........................................

fuerza que empuja desde abajo y que mantiene en el aire a los aviones

## Card 2

the force that pulls all objects toward each other

Write a sentence using this word.

........................................

........................................

........................................

........................................

fuerza que atrae a todos los objetos entre sí

## Card 4

a force that occurs when an object moves through a gas or a liquid

Write a synonym of this word.

........................................

........................................

........................................

fuerza que se produce cuando un objeto se mueve a través de un gas o de un líquido

## Card 7

force that pushes or pulls an airplane forward

Write a sentence using this word.

........................................

........................................

........................................

fuerza que empuja o jala un avión hacia delante

# Chapter 3

# Study Guide

 How can motion be described and measured?

Indiana

### Lesson 1

**What is motion?**

- Objects can move in straight lines or in curved paths.
- Motion is relative and depends on your reference point.
- Objects that do not seem to move form your frame of reference.

### Lesson 2

**What is speed?**

- Speed is the rate at which an object changes position.
- Velocity is both the speed and the direction of a moving object.
- Acceleration is the change in speed or direction of an object.

### Lesson 3

**How do forces affect motion?**

- A force is any push or pull. Forces change the motion of objects.
- Friction tends to slow down objects in motion.
- The balance of lift, drag, thrust, and gravity allows airplanes to fly.

## Lesson 1

### What is motion?

1. **Define** Motion occurs when one object changes _____ relative to another object.
   - A. reference
   - B. position
   - C. force
   - D. time

2. ◉ **Sequence** Read the paragraph. Then, fill in the graphic organizer to show the sequence of events.

> The car that I saw was really cool. First, it came in my direction while I was on the sidewalk. Next, it went past me and messed up my hair. Before going out of sight, it moved away from me.

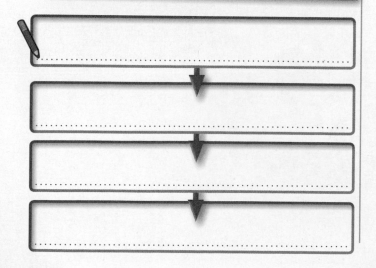

## Lesson 2  ⓓ 4.4.2

### What is speed?

3. **Do the math!** Suppose a car is traveling north on the interstate, and the total distance of the trip is 770 miles. If it takes the car 14 hours to travel the total distance, what is the average speed of the car? Show your work.

_____

_____

_____

_____

4. **Explain** What is velocity?

_____

_____

_____

_____

5. **Apply** Circle the place on the ruler where the marble has the greatest speed.

## Lesson 3  ◑ 4.4.1

### How do forces affect motion?

**6. Explain** Think of an object you use for transportation. Describe how gravity affects the object and how you use the object.

..................................................
..................................................
..................................................
..................................................
..................................................
..................................................

**7. Vocabulary** When Ruben described how the tires on his bicycle skidded on the pavement as he came to a stop, what force was he describing?

A. gravity
B. friction
C. velocity
D. lift

**8. Identify** What forces balance gravity in an airplane and in a boat?

..................................................
..................................................
..................................................

**9.**  **How can motion be described and measured?**

Think about the motion of an airplane. How are speed and acceleration described before takeoff and when an airplane takes off?

..................................................
..................................................
..................................................
..................................................
..................................................
..................................................
..................................................
..................................................
..................................................
..................................................
..................................................
..................................................
..................................................
..................................................

## Multiple Choice

**1** A bicycle uses a force to help control its motion.

What kind of force does a brake apply to the wheel of a bicycle?

   A. gravity

   B. non-contact

   C. pull

   D. friction

**4.4.1**

## Constructed Response

**2** Describe the forces and types of motion that take place in a tug-of-war game.

.......................................................................

.......................................................................

.......................................................................

.......................................................................

.......................................................................

.......................................................................

.......................................................................

**4.4.3**

## Extended Response

**3** Akbar and Logan designed three toy car prototypes in science class. They wanted to find out which car could travel one meter in the shortest amount of time. They tested each car outside on a sidewalk. Their results are shown in the chart below.

| Prototype | Time (seconds) |
|-----------|----------------|
| Car 1 | 2.1 |
| Car 2 | 1.9 |
| Car 3 | 2.4 |

What forces may have affected each car's travel time?

.......................................................................

.......................................................................

.......................................................................

.......................................................................

.......................................................................

Explain why wind may have affected each car's travel time.

.......................................................................

.......................................................................

.......................................................................

.......................................................................

**4.4.2**

4.4.1

# Go Green!

# A Trip to the Indiana Dunes

The Dunes Highway is the name given to a section of United States Highway 12 in Indiana. Part of this highway goes through Indiana Dunes National Lakeshore. Some drivers are cautious and follow the speed limit on this road. Other drivers break the law by driving faster than the speed limit.

There is, however, another reason to travel at or below the speed limit. Did you know that most cars use less gas when they are traveling more slowly? Cars are most efficient when they are moving at a certain speed. A car's gas mileage decreases rapidly when it travels faster than 60 mph. For most cars, the most efficient speed is between 35 and 45 mph.

Place a check mark next to each thing your family does to save fuel.

| Save Fuel in an Automobile |
| --- |
| ☐ Do not accelerate too quickly from stoplights or stop signs. |
| ☐ Keep tires filled with the right amount of air. |
| ☐ Have the vehicle serviced on a regular basis. |
| ☐ Use bicycles or walk when the distance is not far. |

## Inquiry · Design It!

## What design will carry cargo best?

Cargo must be moved from one place to another and delivered on time. Different transportation systems may be used to move the cargo. Many times cargo of different weights and shapes must be moved on trains and trucks. The cargo must be arranged and secured in the vehicle so nothing shifts or falls off. The way the cargo is loaded onto the truck is a design.

You need to design a way to load a group of objects on a cart. Your cargo is a metric ruler, a wooden block, 15 cm of tape, 4 unsharpened pencils, 4 table-tennis balls, a half-full 16 oz. bottle of water, $\frac{1}{2}$ stick of clay, and an inflated balloon. After the cart is loaded you will test your loading design by pulling it through a course your teacher has provided.

## Identify the problem.

☑ **1.** Identify the problems you need to address in your **design.**

.................................................................................................

.................................................................................................

.................................................................................................

.................................................................................................

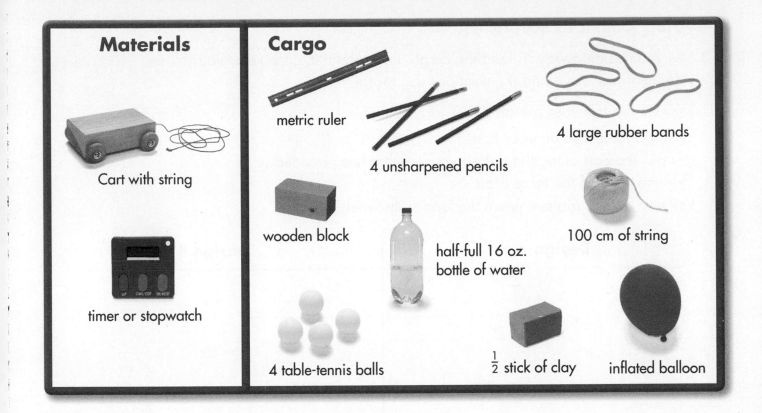

**Materials**

Cart with string

timer or stopwatch

**Cargo**

metric ruler

4 unsharpened pencils

4 large rubber bands

wooden block

half-full 16 oz. bottle of water

100 cm of string

4 table-tennis balls

½ stick of clay

inflated balloon

## Do research.

☑ **2.** Consider the problems you have identified. Research **design** solutions others have used that address those problems. Brainstorm ideas with others. List three examples of solutions others have used or suggested.

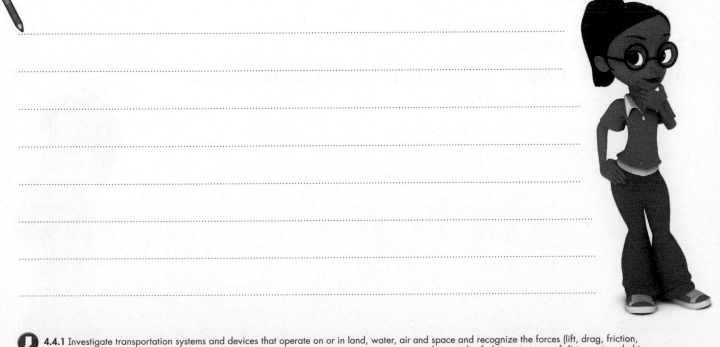

**4.4.1** Investigate transportation systems and devices that operate on or in land, water, air and space and recognize the forces (lift, drag, friction, thrust and gravity) that affect their motion. **4.4.2** Make appropriate measurements to compare the speeds of objects in terms of distance traveled in a given amount of time or time required to travel a given distance. **4.4.3** Investigate how changes in speed or direction are caused by forces; the greater the force exerted on an object, the greater the change. **4.4.4** Define a problem in the context of motion and transportation and propose a solution to this problem by evaluating, reevaluating and testing the design, gathering evidence about how well the design meets the needs of the problem, and documenting the design so that it can be easily replicated. **4.DP.1** Identify a need or problem to be solved. **4.DP.2** Brainstorm potential solutions. **4.DP.3** Document the design throughout the entire design process. **4.DP.4** Select a solution to the need or problem. **4.DP.5** Select the most appropriate materials to develop a solution that will meet the need. **4.DP.6** Create the solution through a prototype. **4.DP.7** Test and evaluate how well the solution meets the goal. **4.DP.8** Evaluate and test the design using measurement. **4.DP.9** Present evidence using mathematical representations (graphs, data tables). **4.DP.10** Communicate the solution including evidence using mathematical representations (graphs, data tables), drawings or prototypes. **4.DP.11** Communicate how to improve the solution.

## Develop possible solutions.

☑ **3.** As you design a way to load the cargo, think about the problems your **design** must solve and the solutions you researched.

When you test your prototype:

- load the cargo on your cart.
- pull the cart along the course your teacher has provided.
- time each of the three trials.
- stop after 3 trials or when the load spills when moving.

| Design A | Design B |
|---|---|
| | |

## Choose one solution.

☑ **4.** Choose one **design** to build and **test.** Tell which design you chose. Explain why you chose that design.

....................................................................................................

....................................................................................................

....................................................................................................

....................................................................................................

110

## Design and construct a prototype.

☑ **5.** Draw the **design** you will use to make a prototype.
Explain why you chose that design.

☑ **6.** Tell how to load the cart.

........................................................................................

........................................................................................

........................................................................................

........................................................................................

........................................................................................

........................................................................................

........................................................................................

........................................................................................

## Test the prototype.

☑ **7.** Test your **design** on the course. Use the timer to record the time it takes to complete one lap of the course.

| | | **Prototype Testing Results** |
|---|---|---|
| **Trial** | **Time** (seconds) | **Notes** |
| 1 | | |
| 2 | | |
| 3 | | |

## Communicate results.

☑ **8.** What elements of your **design** worked in your prototype? Use your **test** results and your **observations** to support your **conclusions**.

..................................................................................................................

..................................................................................................................

..................................................................................................................

..................................................................................................................

☑ **9.** What elements of your design could be improved?

..................................................................................................................

..................................................................................................................

..................................................................................................................

..................................................................................................................

# Evaluate and redesign.

☑ **10.** Evaluate what did and did not work in your prototype.
Use what you learned from testing to **redesign** your prototype.

Write or draw your design changes.

...................................................................................................................................

...................................................................................................................................

...................................................................................................................................

...................................................................................................................................

...................................................................................................................................

## Conduct a Survey

Choose a question to ask each of your classmates. You might ask them what their favorite fruit is or how many pets they have. Collect all the answers. Graph the results of your survey.

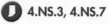 4.NS.3, 4.NS.7

## Write a Report

Choose one kind of transportation system. You may choose airplanes, cars, trucks, or boats. Research how that transportation system has changed society. Write a report about what you learn. Identify the books or other sources in which you found your information.

4.4.1

## Design a Package

Suppose you want to send fresh flowers to a friend. Design a package that will keep the flowers fresh. The flowers and stems should not bend or break. Make sure the flowers can get the light and water that they need.

4.DP.4, 4.DP.5

## Using Scientific Methods

1. Ask a question.
2. State your hypothesis.
3. Identify and control variables.
4. Test your hypothesis.
5. Collect and record your data.
6. Interpret your data.
7. State your conclusion.
8. Try it again.

# Physical
# Science

Chapter 4
## Energy, Heat, and Electricity

THE BIG

How does energy
cause change?

# What puts the BOOM in fireworks?

# Energy, Heat, and Electricity

**Try It!** What can electricity flow through?

**Investigate It!** Which material is the better heat conductor?

When fireworks go off they can be louder than a jet engine. Even if you watch from a safe distance, a fireworks display can be loud enough to make you shake!

**Predict** What forms of energy are at work in a fireworks display?

........................................................................................

........................................................................................

........................................................................................

**THE BIG** How does energy cause change?

## What can electricity flow through?

☑ **1.** Make the circuit as shown.

☑ **2. Predict** Choose one of the objects to complete the circuit. Will it allow the bulb to light up or not? **Record** your predictions for each object.

........................................................................

........................................................................

........................................................................

☑ **3.** Test each object. **Observe.**

*Touch the free ends of the wires to the material being tested.*

**Be careful!** **Wear safety goggles.**

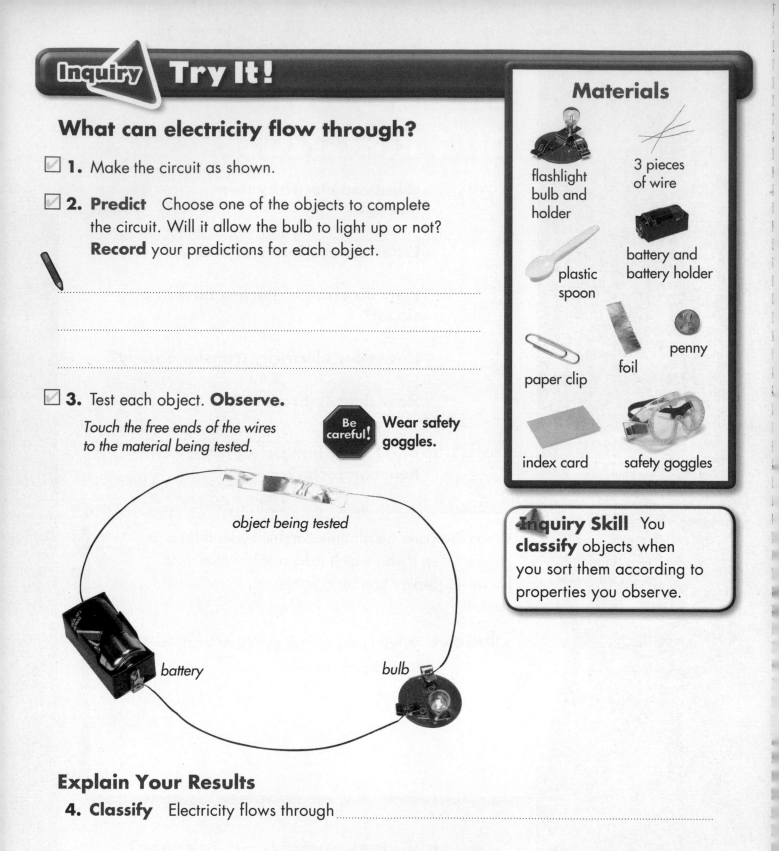

object being tested

battery

bulb

### Materials

flashlight bulb and holder

3 pieces of wire

plastic spoon

battery and battery holder

paper clip

foil

penny

index card

safety goggles

**Inquiry Skill** You **classify** objects when you sort them according to properties you observe.

## Explain Your Results

**4. Classify** Electricity flows through ...........................................

........................................................................

Electricity does not flow through .......................................

........................................................................

**4.1.3** Construct a complete circuit through which an electrical current can pass as evidenced by the lighting of a bulb or ringing of a bell. **4.1.4** Experiment with materials to identify conductors and insulators of heat and electricity. **4.1.5** Demonstrate that electrical energy can be transformed into heat, light, and sound. **4.NS.8** Identify simple patterns in data and propose explanations to account for the patterns. (Also **4.NS.1**)

## ⦿ Main Idea and Details

- The **main idea** is the most important idea in a reading selection.
- **Details** help to explain or support the main idea.

### A Hot Job!

Steelworkers work in one of the world's hottest jobs. At the mill where they work, iron ore is heated with other substances in giant furnaces to become liquid steel. Workers must wear suits that protect them from heat, but they can still sense the warm air around them.

## Practice It!

Complete the graphic organizer below to show the main idea and two details in the example paragraph.

**Main Idea**

..................................................................................
..................................................................................

..................................  ..................................
..................................  ..................................
..................................  ..................................
..................................  ..................................

Detail                              Detail

# What are the forms of energy?

## Envision It!

4.1.1 Describe and investigate the different ways in which heat can be generated.
4.1.5 Demonstrate that electrical energy can be transformed into heat, light, and sound.

**What sounds and movements do you think this plane might make?**

## Inquiry Explore It!

### How can energy change forms?

☑ **1.** Make a circuit. Use wires to connect a battery holder to a light bulb holder.

☑ **2. Observe** In which part of the circuit do you observe light?

...............................................................

☑ **3.** Touch the bulb of the thermometer against the flashlight bulb for 1 minute. What do you observe?

...............................................................

### Explain Your Results

**4. Infer** Tell how energy was transformed to generate heat.

...............................................................

...............................................................

### Materials

safety goggles

2 pieces of insulated wire

flashlight bulb and holder

battery and battery holder

thermometer

**Be careful!** Wear safety goggles.

myscienceonline.com | **Explore It! Animation**

4.1.3 Construct a complete circuit through which an electrical current can pass as evidenced by the lighting of a bulb or ringing of a bell. (Also 4.1.2, 4.NS.4)

## Words to Know

energy
kinetic energy
potential energy

## Energy

Turn on a light switch. Rub your hands together to warm them. Roll a pencil across your desk. You are using energy! **Energy** is the ability to cause motion or create change. Whenever the position, chemical structure, or look of something changes, energy is required.

There are many forms of energy. Some energy takes the form of light or sound. Electrical energy is another type of energy you use every day.

1. ◉ **Main Idea and Details** Complete the graphic organizer below. **Write** details about energy.

2. What is changing about the dog and the toy?

..........................................

..........................................

..........................................

..........................................

..........................................

..........................................

..........................................

**Main Idea**

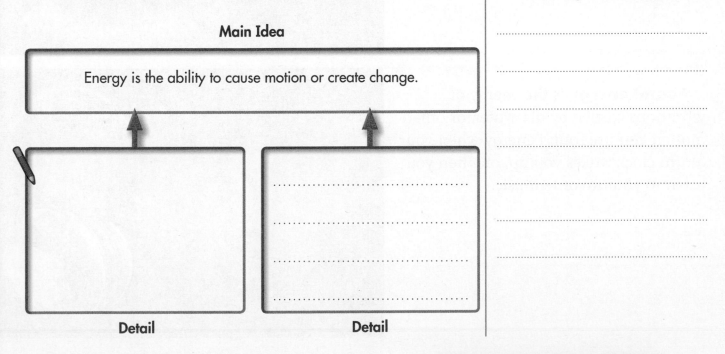

Energy is the ability to cause motion or create change.

Detail                              Detail

# Forms of Energy

Energy cannot be made or destroyed. It is transferred from form to form. Energy also moves from one object to another. Energy can exist in many forms. Here are some common forms of energy.

**Electrical energy** is energy caused by the movement of electrically charged particles. When you flip on a light switch or use a toaster, you are using electrical energy. Electricity flows through the devices to power them.

**3. Describe** Write an example of electrical energy in your home.

........................................................

**Thermal energy** is energy due to the random motion of the particles that make up matter. You can feel the flow of thermal energy as heat. The faster particles move, the more thermal energy is produced. People use thermal energy to heat or cook food. The thermal energy causes changes in the food as it cooks.

**Sound energy** is the energy of vibrations carried by air, water, or other matter. You use sound energy when your alarm clock wakes you up, or when you listen to your favorite music.

**Kinetic energy** is the energy of motion. Anything moving has this kind of energy. A moving swing at the playground and a hurricane both have kinetic energy.

4. **Identify** Write an example of kinetic energy in school.

.................................................................

**Light energy** travels as waves and can move through empty space. Some light energy comes from the sun and travels to Earth. These sunflower plants use this light energy to help make their own food.

**Potential energy** is energy that is stored in an object. When an object is in motion, its potential energy is released as other forms of energy. For example, when a truck burns fuel, the potential energy in gasoline is released as sound, heat, and motion.

5. **Conclude** (Circle) the forms of energy in use when you turn on a fan in your home.

# Where is the energy?

**6.** Look for examples of these forms of energy. Write a total number.

thermal energy .............

sound energy .............

light energy .............

electrical energy .............

kinetic energy .............

## Go Green

**Energy Savers**
Look around your classroom. Describe some forms of energy. How could you save energy? Write a list. Share your list with the school.

## Energy and Motion

All moving things have kinetic energy. The amount of kinetic energy depends on the speed and mass of the object. Look at the photo of the boy tossing an orange. The harder he throws the orange, the more kinetic energy it has. An object with greater mass would also have more kinetic energy.

When the boy throws the orange, he gives it kinetic energy. As the ball rises, it slows down. Its kinetic energy is gradually converted to potential energy. As the orange falls, the potential energy is converted back to kinetic energy.

**7. Explain** Use the photo at left to complete the captions.

## Forms of Potential Energy

There are different forms of potential energy. Some forms have to do with the position of an object. Other forms have to do with the makeup of an object.

## Gravitational

A raised object has what is called gravitational potential energy. The orange the boy is throwing has this kind of potential energy. The higher or heavier an object is, the more gravitational potential energy it has.

**8. Hypothesize** Does the orange have more gravitational potential energy in the boy's hand or high in the air? Explain.

..................................................

..................................................

## Chemical

Chemical potential energy is stored in the connections that hold particles together. A car uses chemical energy when it burns gasoline. The food you eat has chemical energy. When your body digests food, chemical energy turns into other forms of energy that you use to move, talk, and live.

**A** The orange is at rest in the boy's hand. He gives the orange kinetic energy when he throws it.

**B** As the orange rises, its kinetic energy changes to

..................................................

**C** At the top of the throw, the orange has its maximum potential energy.

**D** As the orange falls, its potential energy changes back into

..................................................

### Elastic

A stretched rubber band and a compressed spring have potential energy. This is called elastic potential energy. The more a rubber band is stretched, the more potential energy it has. If you bounce, kick, or hit a ball, the ball also has this kind of potential energy. The ball's material and the air inside it compress like a spring. Elastic potential energy can change into sound energy and kinetic energy.

**9. Hypothesize** Look at the picture of the football. Will its elastic potential energy change into sound energy? Explain.

........................................................

........................................................

........................................................

*The kicker's kinetic energy is transferred to the ball as elastic potential energy. The kick compresses the ball and the air inside it.*

## Got it?

🕐 4.1.5

**10. Categorize** What forms of energy taught in this lesson are produced by a television set?

........................................................

........................................................

**11. Analyze** Suppose you throw a basketball in the air. Instead of catching it, you let it bounce on the court. What kinds of energy are in use as the ball travels?

........................................................

........................................................

⬜ **Stop!** I need help with ........................................................

⏸ **Wait!** I have a question about ........................................................

▶ **Go!** Now I know ........................................................

# Lesson 2

## How do electric charges flow in a circuit?

**4.1.3** Construct a complete circuit through which an electrical current can pass as evidenced by the lighting of a bulb or ringing of a bell.
**4.1.4** Experiment with materials to identify conductors and insulators of heat and electricity.
**4.1.5** Demonstrate that electrical energy can be transformed into heat, light, and sound.

### Envision It!

When you plug a string of light bulbs into an electric outlet, why do you think all the bulbs light up?

## my pLaneT DiaRY

### Science Stats

If you have seen lightning, then you know it can be an incredible sight. Lightning strikes the ground in the United States more than 20 million times in a year. A flash of lightning can heat the air around it to 27,760 degrees Celsius (50,000 degrees Fahrenheit). That is five times hotter than the surface of the sun! One flash of lightning also has enough electricity to light an incandescent light bulb for more than three months.

About how many times has lightning struck the ground since the year you were born?

.........................................................

.........................................................

*Lightning can strike as far as 16 kilometers away from a rainstorm.*

**Words to Know**

| | |
|---|---|
| electric current | series circuit |
| conductor | parallel circuit |
| insulator | |

## Electric Charges

You dash across a carpet and touch a metal doorknob. *Ouch!* A jolt of static electricity startles you. To understand what happened, start with atoms, the tiny building blocks of everything. Most atoms have three types of particles. One type has a positive charge (+). Another type has a negative charge (–). A third type has no charge. Matter usually has the same number of positive and negative particles.

Charged particles can move between objects that are close to each other. Static electricity builds up when positive and negative charges no longer balance. *Static* means "not moving," but eventually the static electricity does move. It may move gradually or it may move very quickly. Moving charges generate electrical energy, which can change into sound energy, light energy, or heat.

2. **Infer** Name an object that may have caused the static electricity in this child's hair.

.........................................................

.........................................................

1. ⊚ **Cause and Effect** Complete the graphic organizer below. Write the cause of static electricity.

**Cause**

**Effect**

Static electricity builds up.

Look at objects at your desk and around your classroom. Think about what material each object is made of. Make a list of objects that are conductors and a list of objects that are insulators.

## How Electric Charges Flow

Most electricity is on the go. An electric charge in motion is called an **electric current**. An electric current flows quickly and invisibly from one place to another.

### Conductors

The flow of electric charge is not the same in all materials. Some kinds of atoms become charged more easily than others. Materials made of easily charged atoms are conductors. A **conductor** is a material through which an electric charge can move easily. Most metals, such as copper, gold, and silver, are good conductors. Other conductors include metal scissors and the pencil lead, or graphite, in your pencil.

3. ◎ **Cause and Effect** In the text, **underline** what causes some materials to be good conductors of electricity.

4. **Explain** The computer part below is made of gold conductors. Will gold allow electric charges to flow easily in this computer part? Why or Why not?

........................................................................

........................................................................

## Insulators

Other materials are made of atoms that do not become charged easily. An **insulator** is a material through which an electric charge moves with difficulty. Plastic, rubber, glass, and dry wood are good insulators. Other insulators are the eraser on your pencil and the chalk you may use to draw.

5. **Analyze** Why are glass insulators used on power lines?

..................................................................................

..................................................................................

glass insulators

6. **Infer** Electricians often wear special shoes with thick, rubber soles. Why?

..................................................................................

..................................................................................

..................................................................................

*plastic insulator*

*conductor*

The plug and the wires inside this electrical cord are conductors. The plastic insulator makes the cord safe to handle.

## Circuits

For a current to flow, electric charges must complete a loop, or circuit. A current cannot flow if the circuit has any gaps, or breaks. A cut wire and an off switch are examples of breaks. A circuit is open if it has at least one break. It is closed if it has no breaks. For example, if a switch in a flashlight is turned off, the circuit is open.

A circuit has many parts. Its energy source provides the energy to move electric charges. Batteries and electrical outlets are energy sources. A circuit has wires through which the charges flow. It also has resistors such as light bulbs or machines. Resistors transform electrical energy to other forms of energy. They use the energy that flows through the circuit. A circuit may also have a switch. The symbols below are used to represent the parts of a circuit.

**CIRCUIT SYMBOLS**

Switch

Energy Source

Resistor

**7. Conclude** Think about what you read about series circuits. Why are the bulbs in the series circuit above not lit?

........................................................

........................................................

## Series Circuits

One type of circuit is called a series circuit. In a **series circuit**, electric charge can flow in only one circular path. When the power source is turned on, the charged particles in the wire flow in one direction around a single loop. Any break in the loop, such as a burnt-out or missing bulb, stops the current from flowing.

**8. Recognize** Label the parts of this series circuit.

........................................................

........................................................

## Parallel Circuits

Another type of circuit is a parallel circuit. A **parallel circuit** has two or more paths through which electric charges may flow. Each path leaves from the power source and returns to it. The current that flows through one path does not have to flow through the other paths. Therefore, if one loop in the circuit is broken, the current will still flow through the other loops.

**9. Locate** (Circle) the loop that is broken.

*In a parallel circuit, one missing or burnt-out bulb does not open the circuit.*

## Got it?

🔘 4.1.3, 4.1.4

**10. Classify** How can you classify materials as conductors or insulators?

.................................................................

.................................................................

**11. 🔘 Cause and Effect** Explain how a switch can affect the flow of an electric current in a circuit.

.................................................................

.................................................................

.................................................................

⏹ **Stop!** I need help with ..........................

⏸ **Wait!** I have a question about ......................

▶ **Go!** Now I know ......................................

**Lesson 3**

# How does electricity transfer energy?

4.1.5 Demonstrate that electrical energy can be transformed into heat, light, and sound.

## Envision It!

How is electricity important to the plants in this tank?

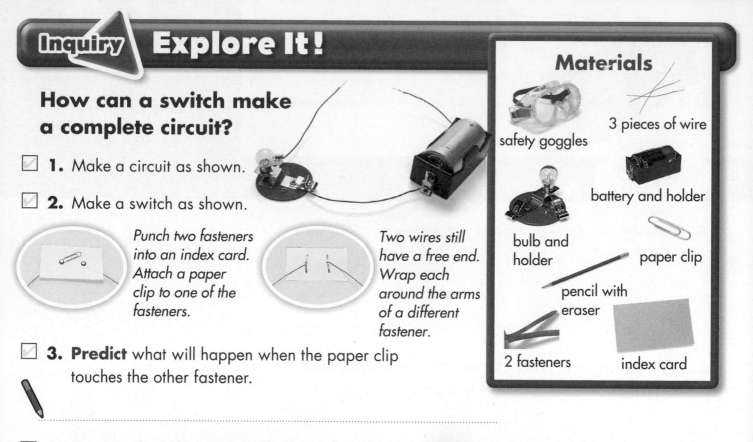

## Inquiry Explore It!

### How can a switch make a complete circuit?

☑ **1.** Make a circuit as shown.

☑ **2.** Make a switch as shown.

*Punch two fasteners into an index card. Attach a paper clip to one of the fasteners.*

*Two wires still have a free end. Wrap each around the arms of a different fastener.*

☑ **3. Predict** what will happen when the paper clip touches the other fastener.

☑ **4.** Use the pencil eraser to touch the paper clip to the other fastener. **Observe.**

 **Be careful!** Wear safety goggles.

### Materials

safety goggles

3 pieces of wire

battery and holder

bulb and holder

paper clip

pencil with eraser

2 fasteners

index card

### Explain Your Results

**5. Draw a Conclusion** How did the paper clip act as a switch?

myscienceonline.com | xplore It! Animation

4.1.3 Construct a complete circuit through which an electrical current can pass as evidenced by the lighting of a bulb or ringing of a bell. (Also **4.NS.1, 4.NS.9**)

UNLOCK
THE BIG

I will know how energy changes form. I will know how electricity changes to light and gives off heat.

**Word to Know**

filament

## Energy Changing Form

Energy is never lost. It cannot be made or destroyed. However, energy can transform, or change form. Electrical, light, sound, thermal, potential, and kinetic energy are all forms of energy. Electrical energy can change to light energy. Kinetic energy can change to sound energy or electrical energy. These examples are only some ways that energy can change.

Many objects transform energy as they work. A lamp transforms electrical energy to light energy. If you pluck a guitar string, the kinetic energy of the string transforms to sound energy. A wind turbine transforms kinetic energy to electrical energy.

You experience energy changing form when you rub your hands together quickly. The kinetic energy of your hands' motion causes friction. Friction is a force that acts when two surfaces rub together. As a result of friction, kinetic energy changes to thermal energy, and heat is given off. So, your hands warm up.

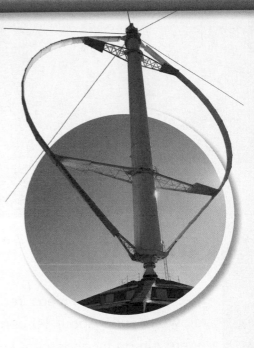

*A wind turbine transforms energy.*

1. **Exemplify** Name an object that transforms electrical energy to sound energy.

....................................................

2. **Recognize** Write how energy is transformed by a wind turbine.

.........................................

energy changes to

.........................................

## Light from Electricity

Televisions, computers, and light bulbs all use electricity. These objects are resistors that use the energy in a circuit. Most resistors transform electrical energy to heat and light. The filament in an incandescent light bulb is its resistor. A **filament** is a thin, coiled wire that can get very hot without melting. Most of the electricity passing through the filament is changed into heat. But the filament is a strong resistor. The filament becomes so hot that it glows, also giving off light.

3. Cause and Effect
   **Underline** the cause of electricity being changed into light in a filament.

*incandescent light bulb*

*fluorescent light bulb*

## Heat from Electricity

When electrical current passes through a resistor, it often gives off heat. This change is why electrical wires sometimes become hot. Some types of wires are good resistors. Many appliances have coils of these wires. More coils allow an appliance to become hotter. The resistors of some appliances get so hot that they produce a red glow. This glow happens in toasters.

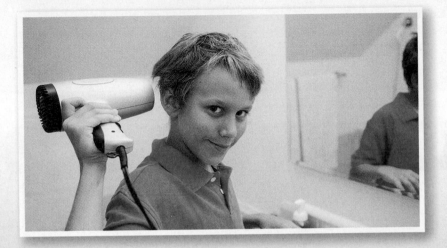

## At-Home Lab

**Motion and Heat**
Rub an eraser quickly across a table several times. Touch the eraser. Then describe how it feels.

4. **Infer** Many hair dryers use heating coils as resistors. Explain why.

........................................................

........................................................

## Got it?

🔾 4.1.5

5. **Summarize** Describe how a filament in an incandescent light bulb transforms electrical energy.

........................................................

........................................................

........................................................

6. **UNLOCK THE BIG** How can objects transform electrical energy?

........................................................

........................................................

........................................................

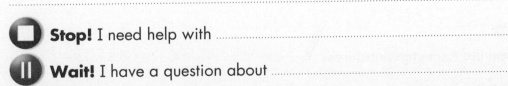

⬜ **Stop!** I need help with ........................................................

⏸ **Wait!** I have a question about ........................................................

▶ **Go!** Now I know ........................................................

# Lesson 4

## How does heat move?

**4.1.1** Describe and investigate the different ways in which heat can be generated.

**4.1.2** Investigate the variety of ways that heat can be generated and move from one place to another and explain the direction in which the heat moves.

### Envision It!

In this kind of photograph, different temperatures show up as different colors.

---

## Inquiry Explore It!

### How does heat move?

1. Fill a paper cup with warm water. Cover it. Push a thermometer through the lid and hold it in place with clay. **Record** the temperature. .................°C.

2. Fill a foam cup $\frac{1}{4}$ full with very cold water. Record the temperature. .................°C.

3. Place the paper cup inside the foam cup. Record the temperature in each cup every minute for 10 minutes.

### Materials

paper cup with lid    foam cup

clay    2 thermometers

clock with a second hand    warm water    very cold water

### Heat Movement Observations

| | Water Temperature (°C) | | | | | | | | | | |
|---|---|---|---|---|---|---|---|---|---|---|---|
| | Start | 1 min | 2 min | 3 min | 4 min | 5 min | 6 min | 7 min | 8 min | 9 min | 10 min |
| Paper Cup | | | | | | | | | | | |
| Foam Cup | | | | | | | | | | | |

## Explain Your Results

4. **Observe** What happened to the temperatures? ...............................

5. **Infer** Tell which way heat moves between objects with different temperatures.

myscienceonline.com | Explore It! Animation

**4.NS.5** Use measurement skills and apply appropriate units when collecting data. (Also **4.1.4, 4.NS.7, 4.NS.8, 4.DP.9**)

**Which colors do you think represent warmer areas?**

I will know that heat flows from hot objects to cold ones. I will know that some materials are good conductors of heat and others are not.

**Words to Know**

conduction
convection
radiation

## Conduction

Thermal energy flows from something warm to something cool. The transfer of thermal energy between matter of different temperatures is heat. A heat source is anything that gives off energy that particles of matter can take in.

When you go to bed at night, does your pillow feel cool on your face? Is the pillow warm when you wake up? That is thermal energy moving! Your body is the heat source. Thermal energy transfers from your body to your pillow. When solids touch, thermal energy moves by conduction. **Conduction** is the transfer of heat that occurs when one thing touches another.

A bird warming her eggs in a nest is another example of conduction. The bird's body is the heat source. Conduction transfers thermal energy from the bird to the cooler eggs.

1. **Visualize** Draw an ice cube sitting on a counter top on a hot day. Draw an arrow showing which direction thermal energy flows.

## At-Home Lab

**Heat on the Move**
Put a thermometer in various places around your home. Record your findings. Think about why some places are cooler or warmer than others. Where might heat be moving in or out of a home?

## A Conduction Example

Have you ever eaten hot oatmeal for breakfast? Suppose that you eat a bowl of hot oatmeal with a metal spoon. Why does the metal spoon begin to feel warmer? The particles of the spoon that touch the oatmeal start to move faster. As they move more quickly, they crash into other particles in the spoon. Thermal energy from the oatmeal moves throughout the spoon. Heat transfer continues until the oatmeal and the spoon are the same temperature.

2. **Infer** How do you know that heat from the oatmeal has moved?

...........................................................................

...........................................................................

...........................................................................

...........................................................................

3. **Decide** Suppose cold milk is poured into a warm glass. What will happen to the milk's temperature? Why?

..................................

..................................

..................................

..................................

..................................

..................................

..................................

..................................

..................................

140

## Conductors

### Iron

Some materials allow heat to move through them more easily than others do. These materials are called conductors. A conductor is a material that readily allows heat to move—like this iron frying pan. Many metals, such as iron and aluminum, conduct heat well.

4. **Predict** If you place an iron pan on a burner or other heat source, what will happen?

### Copper

Did you take a hot shower today? Your water may have been heated using copper. Copper is another metal that is an excellent conductor. Many water heaters use copper coils to heat water. An outside heat source heats the metal. Then the water circulates around the coils to heat up.

## Insulators

### Wood

Some things—like a wooden spoon—do not get too warm even when they touch something hot. These materials are insulators. An insulator is a material that limits the amount of heat that passes through it.

5. **Analyze** Why do you think many cooks in pizza restaurants use wooden paddles to remove hot pizzas from the oven?

### Plastic

Do you know why so many foods are served in foam containers? The plastic foam used to make the containers has many small air pockets in it. The plastic is a good insulator. Air is a good insulator too. The plastic and the trapped air keep the food at the right temperature.

# Convection

Have you felt how warm a kitchen gets when the oven is on? The warmth throughout the room is the result of convection. **Convection** is the transfer of thermal energy as matter moves. In convection, a gas or a liquid moves from place to place. The oven heats air inside it. Particles in the warm air move faster and travel upward into the rest of the kitchen. Then cooler air enters the oven to be warmed up. The greenhouse below shows another example of convection.

A pattern of flowing matter carrying thermal energy is called a convection current. A convection current forms when gas or liquid transfers heat as it moves.

**6. Summarize** Complete the captions below.

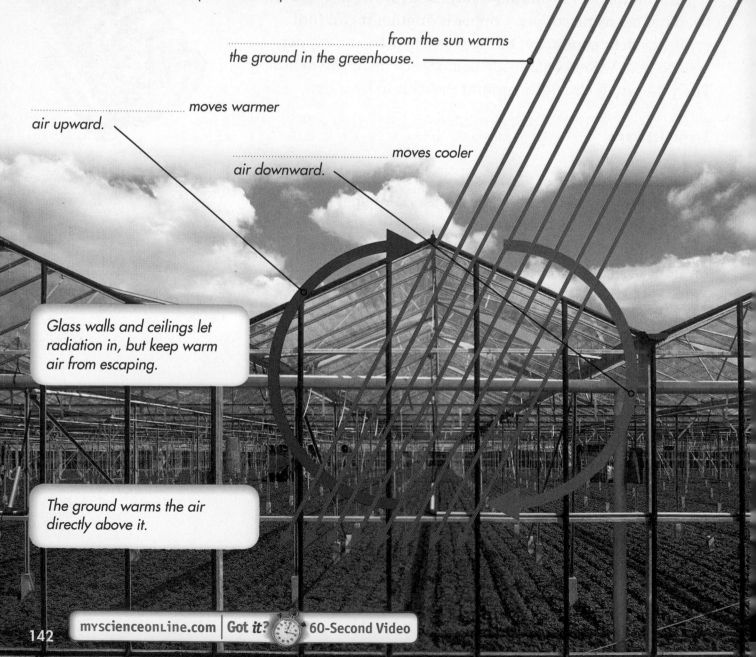

.................................................... from the sun warms the ground in the greenhouse.

.................................................... moves warmer air upward.

.................................................... moves cooler air downward.

Glass walls and ceilings let radiation in, but keep warm air from escaping.

The ground warms the air directly above it.

myscienceonline.com | Got it? 60-Second Video

# Radiation

When the sun warms your skin or you sit near a fire, you feel another kind of energy. This energy is radiant energy, or radiation. **Radiation** is energy that is sent out in waves. When radiant energy hits you, the particles in your skin move more quickly. The radiation is converted to thermal energy and you feel warm.

Radiation transfers heat differently than conduction or convection. Conduction and convection both need the particles in matter to transfer heat. But radiation does not need particles. It can travel without them. Radiation can travel through matter and through empty space.

7. [CHALLENGE] How might the sun's radiation cause conduction and convection?

.......................................................................

.......................................................................

## Got it?  4.1.2

8. **Classify** How is thermal energy transferred to you in these situations?

The sun warms your head at the beach. ...............................

You eat a warm bite of food. .................................................

After you get out of a long shower, the bathroom is warm. ...............

9.  **UNLOCK THE BIG Q** Think about what you have read in this lesson. How does energy create change?

.......................................................................

.......................................................................

⬛ **Stop!** I need help with ..................................................

⏸ **Wait!** I have a question about ......................................

▶ **Go!** Now I know .............................................................

## Which material is the better heat conductor?

### Follow a Procedure

☑ **1.** Place $\frac{1}{4}$ of a spoonful of margarine on the handles of each spoon. Stick a bead into the margarine on each spoon. Place both spoons in an empty cup.

☑ **2.** Pick up the cup filled halfway with very warm water. Gently pour it into the cup with the spoons.

**Materials**

2 small beads          margarine

metal spoon

plastic spoon

plastic cup $\frac{1}{2}$ full of very warm water

timer, stopwatch, or clock with second hand

empty plastic cup

**Be careful!** Use water that is a safe temperature.

**Inquiry Skill**
Carrying out an investigation carefully and observing closely, helps you make accurate **inferences.**

**4.1.2** Investigate the variety of ways that heat can be generated and move from one place to another and explain the direction in which the heat moves. **4.1.4** Experiment with materials to identify conductors and insulators of heat and electricity. **4.NS.8** Identify simple patterns in data and propose explanations to account for the patterns. (Also **4.NS.1**)

☑ **3. Observe** Watch the beads closely. Time how long it takes for each bead to fall.

☑ **4. Record** your **data** below.

| Heat Conductor Observations | |
|---|---|
| Material | Observations and Melting Time |
| Plastic spoon | |
| Metal spoon | |

## Analyze and Conclude

**5.** Write an explanation for your **observations.**

........................................................................................

........................................................................................

........................................................................................

**6. Infer** Which of the materials would be better for a cooking pot? Explain how you made your inference.

........................................................................................

........................................................................................

........................................................................................

**7.** UNLOCK THE BIG Q  What do your observations teach you about how energy moves?

........................................................................................

........................................................................................

........................................................................................

# Electrician

You flip a switch and a light goes on. Every time this happens, you have an electrician to thank.

Electricians run the wires that carry current throughout your home, your school, and any building that has electricity. Some electricians work mainly in houses and other small buildings. Others work in office buildings, where they might install telephones and cables for computers as well as electrical wiring. Still others work in large factories, where they might repair robots or fix machine tools.

Electricians check to make sure that electrical systems are safe. They usually spend much of the workday on their feet. Sometimes they need to climb ladders or crawl into small spaces to put up or repair wires. They must work carefully because poor wiring can cause electrical shocks and fires.

If you like to work with your hands and are good at problem solving, you might like to become an electrician.

**Apply** Why do you think it is important for electricians to be good at problem solving?

........................................................................

........................................................................

........................................................................

# Vocabulary Smart Cards

energy
kinetic energy
potential energy
electric current
conductor
insulator
series circuit
parallel circuit
filament
conduction
convection
radiation

## Play a Game!

Cut out the Vocabulary Smart Cards.

Work with a partner. Choose a Vocabulary Smart Card. Do not let your partner see your card.

Draw a picture to show what the word means. Have your partner guess the word. Take turns drawing and guessing.

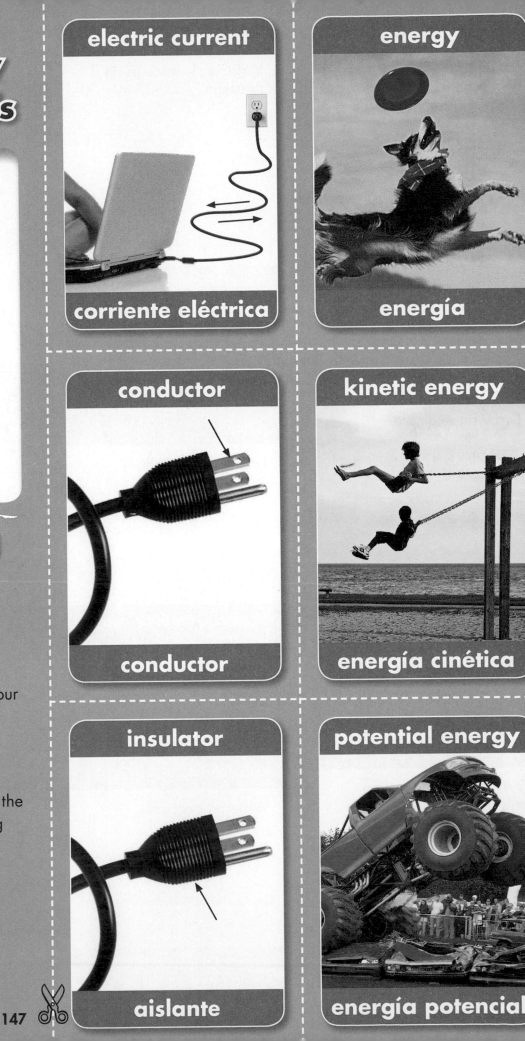

**electric current**

corriente eléctrica

**energy**

energía

**conductor**

conductor

**kinetic energy**

energía cinética

**insulator**

aislante

**potential energy**

energía potencial

the ability to cause motion or create change

Write an example.

.......................................

.......................................

.......................................

.......................................

capacidad de producir movimiento o causar cambio

---

an electric charge in motion

Write a sentence using this term.

.......................................

.......................................

.......................................

carga eléctrica en movimiento

---

Gold is one of the best conductors.

conductor material through which an electric charge can move easily

## Make a Word Pyramid!

Choose a vocabulary word and write the word and definition in the base of the pyramid. Write a sentence in the middle of the pyramid. Draw a picture of an example, or of something related, at the top.

---

energy of motion

Draw an example.

energía de movimiento

---

a material through which an electric charge can move easily

Draw an example.

material a través del cual las cargas eléctricas se mueven fácilmente

---

energy that is stored in an object

Write a sentence using this term.

.......................................

.......................................

.......................................

.......................................

energía que está almacenada en un objeto

---

a material through which an electric charge moves with difficulty

Write an example.

.......................................

.......................................

.......................................

material a través del cual las cargas elécticas se mueven con dificultad

| | **conduction** | **series circuit** |
|---|---|---|
| | 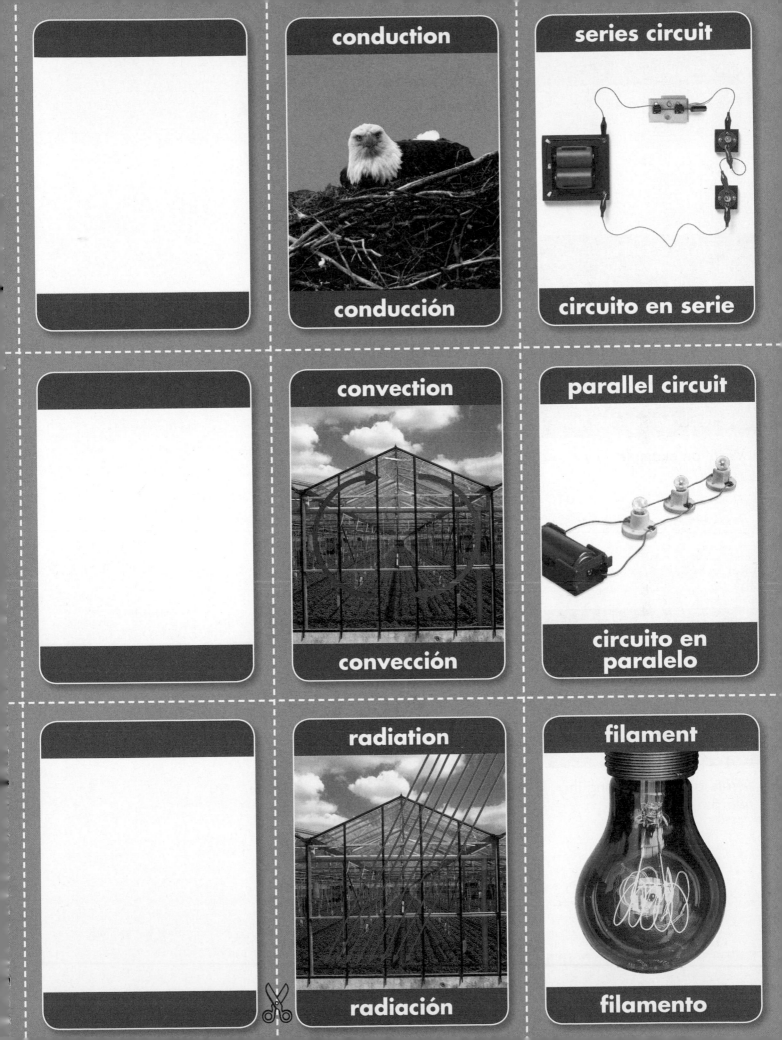 | |
| | **conducción** | **circuito en serie** |
| | **convection** | **parallel circuit** |
| | | |
| | **convección** | **circuito en paralelo** |
| | **radiation** | **filament** |
| | | |
| | **radiación** | **filamento** |

a circuit in which electrical charge can only flow in one circular path

Draw an example.

circuito en el cual las cargas eléctricas sólo pueden fluir en una trayectoria circular

the transfer of heat that occurs when one thing touches another

Write a sentence using the verb form of this word.

.................................................

.................................................

.................................................

transmisión de calor que ocurre cuando un objeto toca otro objeto

a circuit that has two or more paths through which electrical charges may flow

Write an example.

.................................................

.................................................

.................................................

circuito que tiene dos o más vías por las que pueden fluir las cargas eléctricas

the transfer of thermal energy as matter moves

Write an example.

.................................................

.................................................

.................................................

.................................................

transferencia de energía térmica mientras se mueve la materia

a thin, coiled wire that can get very hot without melting

Write a sentence using this word.

.................................................

.................................................

.................................................

alambre fino y enrollado que puede calentarse mucho sin derretirse

energy that is sent out in waves

Write a sentence using the verb form of this word.

.................................................

.................................................

.................................................

energía transmitida a través de ondas

### Lesson 1

**What are the forms of energy?**

- The common forms of energy are electrical energy, thermal energy, sound energy, kinetic energy, light energy, and potential energy.
- Energy is the ability to cause motion or create change.

### Lesson 2

**How do electric charges flow in a circuit?**

- An electric charge flows through conductors easily.
- An electric charge flows through insulators with difficulty.
- For a current to flow, electric charges must complete a circuit.

### Lesson 3

**How does electricity transfer energy?**

- Kinetic energy can cause friction and give off heat.
- Electrical energy can change to light energy and give off heat.

### Lesson 4

**How does heat move?**

- Heat is the transfer of thermal energy.
- Heat can move by conduction, convection, or radiation.

# Chapter Review

 How does energy cause change?

## Lesson 1  • 4.1.1, 4.1.5

### What are the forms of energy?

1. **Vocabulary** The energy of motion is called
   A. potential energy.
   B. kinetic energy.
   C. chemical energy.
   D. thermal energy.

2. **Analyze** What two kinds of energy are you using when you play on a slide?

## Lesson 2  • 4.1.3, 4.1.4, 4.1.5

### How do electric charges flow in a circuit?

3. ◉ **Cause and Effect** Circle a cause and **underline** its effect in the paragraph below.

   Electric charges move more easily through some materials than others. Conductors are materials with atoms that easily become charged. As a result, an electric charge can move easily through a conductor. Most metals are good conductors.

4. **Predict** Suppose you have a set of lights that are wired in a parallel circuit. What will happen to the circuit if one bulb burns out?

5. **Write About It** A flashlight is a series circuit that has a battery as its energy source. Describe what happens in a flashlight when the switch is turned from *off* to *on*.

## Lesson 3   🟡 4.1.5

**How does electricity transfer energy?**

6. **Vocabulary** The resistor in an incandescent light bulb is called
   A. an insulator.
   B. an electric charge.
   C. a filament.
   D. a power source.

7. **Apply** List three appliances that transform electrical energy into another form of energy. Identify the form or forms of energy each produces.

.............................................................

.............................................................

.............................................................

.............................................................

.............................................................

**Do the math!**

8. **Calculate** About 75 percent of the energy that passes through a fluorescent bulb becomes light. If a fluorescent bulb uses 2,000 kilowatt-hours, how much energy becomes light?

.............................................................

.............................................................

.............................................................

## Lesson 4   🟡 4.1.1, 4.1.2

**How does heat move?**

9. **Explain** When two solids touch, thermal energy transfers from one solid to the other by
   A. insulation.
   B. radiation.
   C. conduction.
   D. convection.

10. **Analyze** Which of these items is the best conductor of heat?
    A. A metal fork
    B. A wooden drawer handle
    C. A solid plastic ladle
    D. A foam plastic drink container

11. **APPLY THE BIG** **How does energy cause change?**

    ...................................................

    Think back to this morning as you were getting ready for school. Name some of the different forms of energy you used or saw. How did you use them?

    .............................................................

    .............................................................

    .............................................................

    .............................................................

## Multiple Choice

**1** A material through which an electric charge can move easily is

  A. a resistor

  B. an insulator

  C. a filament

  D. a conductor  **◗ 4.1.3**

## Constructed Response

**2** How does energy change as it moves through this circuit?

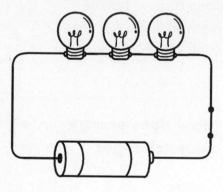

**◗ 4.1.5**

## Extended Response

**3** Marques and his family use electricity to power many of the things they use at home. The chart below shows how much of the total electricity each item uses.

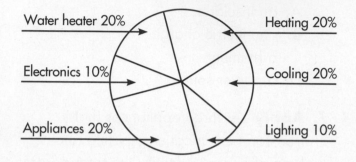

Which sections are likely to include electricity usage in the living room?

How much of the total electricity do heating, cooling, and appliances use?

Describe one change Marques might make and how it would affect this chart.

**◗ 4.1.5**

# UNPLUG IT!

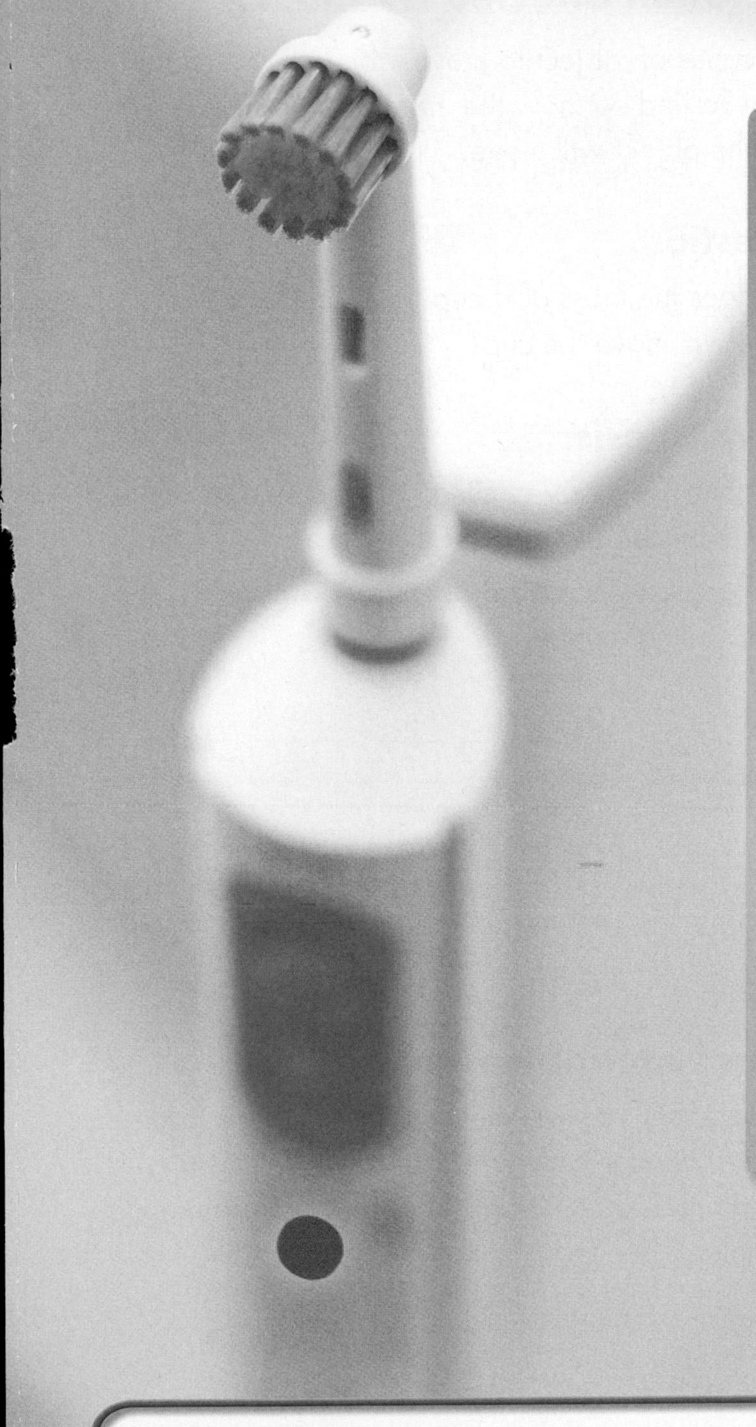

Did you know that a television continues to use energy, even when it is turned off? Computers, cell phone chargers, and electric toothbrushes do too. These devices continue to use energy because they are still plugged into a power source. The energy that flows through them, even when they are off, is called phantom energy. Phantom energy makes up part of a household's energy use. A household may spend about $100 each year on phantom energy.

You can make a difference. To conserve energy, plug your computer and other electronics into a power strip. When you are not using the electronics, switch off the power strip. Or unplug the electronics altogether. This simple step will stop phantom energy from flowing. Conserving energy will help the environment. It will also save your family money.

**Analyze** The toothbrush in the picture above is turned off. How can you tell that it is still using energy?

## Materials

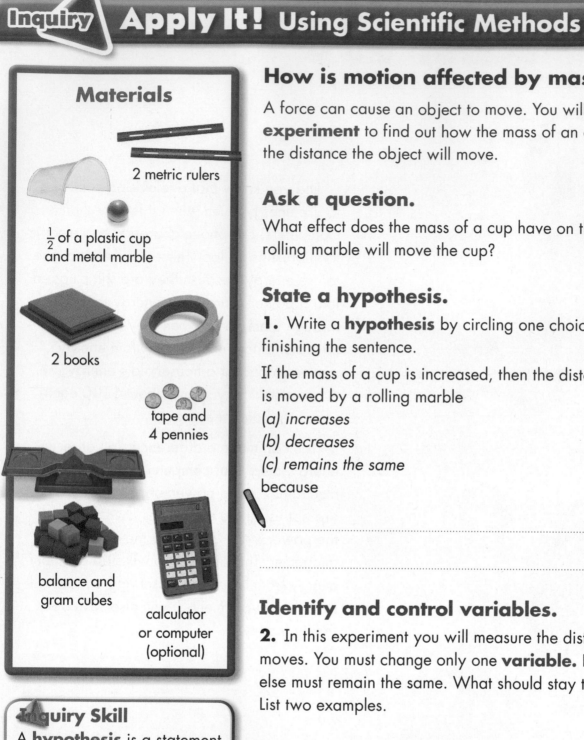

2 metric rulers

$\frac{1}{2}$ of a plastic cup and metal marble

2 books

tape and 4 pennies

balance and gram cubes

calculator or computer (optional)

### Inquiry Skill

A **hypothesis** is a statement that explains an observation. It can be tested by an experiment.

## How is motion affected by mass?

A force can cause an object to move. You will conduct an **experiment** to find out how the mass of an object affects the distance the object will move.

## Ask a question.

What effect does the mass of a cup have on the distance a rolling marble will move the cup?

## State a hypothesis.

**1.** Write a **hypothesis** by circling one choice and finishing the sentence.

If the mass of a cup is increased, then the distance the cup is moved by a rolling marble

*(a) increases*

*(b) decreases*

*(c) remains the same*

because

............................................................................

............................................................................

## Identify and control variables.

**2.** In this experiment you will measure the distance the cup moves. You must change only one **variable.** Everything else must remain the same. What should stay the same? List two examples.

............................................................................

............................................................................

**3.** Tell the one change you will make.

............................................................................

............................................................................

............................................................................

 **4.4.3** Investigate how changes in speed or direction are caused by forces; the greater the force exerted on an object, the greater the change.
**4.NS.7** Keep accurate records in a notebook during investigations and communicate findings to others using graphs, charts, maps and models through oral and written reports. (Also **4.DP.9, 4.NS.5**)

## Design your test.

☑ **4.** Draw how you will set up your test.

☑ **5.** List your steps in the order you will do them.

## Do your test.

☑ **6.** Follow the steps you wrote.

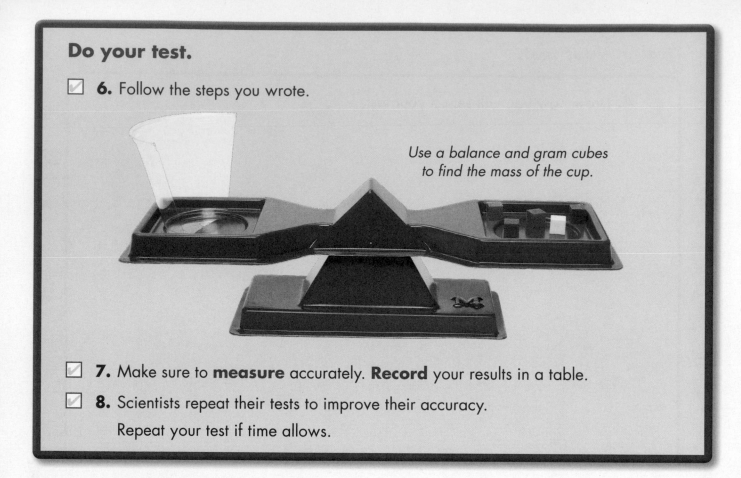

*Use a balance and gram cubes to find the mass of the cup.*

☑ **7.** Make sure to **measure** accurately. **Record** your results in a table.

☑ **8.** Scientists repeat their tests to improve their accuracy. Repeat your test if time allows.

## Collect and record your data.

☑ **9.** Fill in the chart.

| | | |
|---|---|---|
| | | |
| | | |
| | | |
| | | |
| | | |
| | | |

**Work Like a Scientist**
Clear and active communication is an essential part of doing science. Talk with your classmates. Compare your methods and results.

## Interpret your data.

☑ **10.** Use your data to make a line graph.

☑ **11.** Look at your graph closely. Describe how the distance the cup moved was affected by the mass of the cup. Identify the evidence you used to answer the question.

...........................................................................

...........................................................................

...........................................................................

...........................................................................

...........................................................................

**Technology Tools**
Your teacher may wish to have you use a computer (with the right software) or a graphing calculator to help collect, organize, analyze, and present your data. These tools can help you make tables, charts, and graphs.

## State your conclusion.

**12. Communicate** your conclusion. Compare your **hypothesis** with your results. Compare your results with those of others.

...........................................................................

...........................................................................

...........................................................................

...........................................................................

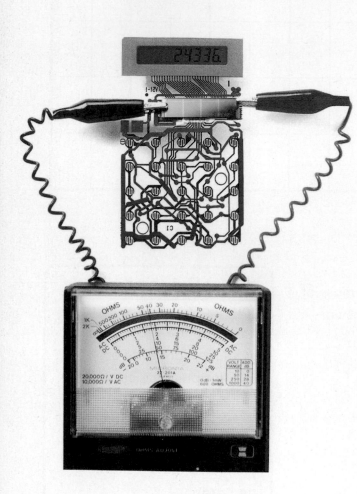

## Using Scientific Methods

1. Ask a question.
2. State your hypothesis.
3. Identify and control variables.
4. Test your hypothesis.
5. Collect and record your data.
6. Interpret your data.
7. State your conclusion.
8. Try it again.

## Height and Potential Energy

Find out how the height of an object affects its potential energy. Use modeling clay to make three balls of the same size. Place a ball in a plastic bag and put it on the floor. Hold a thick book flat above the ball. Release the book so it lands on the clay. Remove the flattened ball from the bag and trace its outline on a sheet of paper. Repeat the procedure using the other balls of clay, but drop the book from different heights. Record your procedures and your observations. Draw conclusions based on your information.

🅘 4.NS.4

## Energy into Electricity

Just as electricity can be transformed into other forms of energy, other forms of energy can be turned into electricity. Write about three different forms of energy that have been used to produce electricity: wind turbines, solar panels, nuclear reactors, hydroelectric dams, geothermal power plants, or any others that you can find out about.

🅘 4.1.5

## Write a Poem

Write a poem about conductors and insulators. Include some examples of each type of material. Tell how they may be useful or dangerous. Here are some tips to help you write your poem:

- A poem often has words that repeat.
- The words can be recited in rhythm, and they often rhyme.

🅘 4.1.4

# Earth Science

Chapter 5
## Earth's Changing Surface

How do Earth's resources change?

# How can magma form steps?

# Earth's Changing Surface

**Try It!** How can a landslide shape the land?

**Lesson 1** What are weathering and erosion?
4.2.1, 4.2.2

**Lesson 2** What are the properties of soil?
4.2.1

**Lesson 3** How does Earth's surface change rapidly?
4.2.3

**Lesson 4** How do people change Earth's surface?
4.2.6

**Lesson 5** What are natural resources?
4.2.4, 4.2.5

**Investigate It!** Why are earth materials important?

Giant's Causeway is a formation of about 40,000 stone pillars in Northern Ireland. The tops of the pillars form a path of steppingstones to the sea. Cooling magma from an ancient volcano formed Giant's Causeway between 50 and 60 million years ago.

**Predict** What forces might have shaped this formation?

..................................................................................................

..................................................................................................

**THE BIG Q** How do Earth's resources change?

## How can a landslide shape the land?

☑ **1. Make a Model** Make a slope in the plastic tub with the sand.

☑ **2.** Place gram cubes at the top and bottom of the slope to represent houses. Draw and label a side view.

**Before**

### Materials

container with moist sand

4 gram cubes

paper cup with holes

paper cup with water

**Inquiry Skill**
**Making a model** can help you understand natural events.

☑ **3.** Hold the paper cup with holes over the top of the slope. Pour water from the other paper cup into the paper cup with holes. **Observe.** Draw and label a side view.

**After**

## Explain Your Results

4. **UNLOCK THE BIG** **Draw a Conclusion** Based on your model, describe how a landslide can change the shape of the land. How might houses be affected?

4.2.2 Demonstrate and describe how wind, water and glacial ice shape and reshape earth's land surface by eroding rock and soil in some areas and depositing them in other areas in a process that occurs over a long period of time. 4.2.3 Demonstrate and describe how earthquakes, volcanoes, and landslides suddenly change the shape of the land. (Also 4.NS.7, 4.NS.8)

## Draw Conclusions

- A **conclusion** is a decision you reach after you think about observations and data that you know or have gathered.
- The conclusion should make sense and be supported by the facts.

### Glaciers

Huge ice sheets called glaciers have covered vast areas of Earth's surface for millions of years. Most glaciers move very slowly. Though the ice of a glacier is solid, it can still move. As the glacier flows and slides over the ground, it wears away bits of rock and soil. Even small glaciers can rip rocks apart and carry large chunks for long distances.

## Practice It!

Complete the graphic organizer. Read the three facts about glaciers from the paragraph above. Then write a conclusion.

| Facts | Conclusion |
|---|---|
| Most glaciers move very slowly. | |
| Glaciers wear away rock and soil as they move. | |
| Glaciers can rip rocks apart and carry large chunks for long distances. | |

# What are weathering and erosion?

4.2.1 Demonstrate and describe how smaller rocks come from the breakage and weathering of larger rocks in a process that occurs over a long period of time. 4.2.2 Demonstrate and describe how wind, water and glacial ice shape and reshape earth's land surface by eroding rock and soil in some areas and depositing them in other areas in a process that occurs over a long period of time.

## Envision It!

Tell what you think is shaping this beach.

## Inquiry Explore It!

### How does a rock wear away?

☑ **1.** Shake chalk and rocks in a jar for 1 minute. Look for changes in the chalk. Shake for 3 more minutes. **Observe.**

☑ **2.** Empty the jar. Fill it half full with water. Repeat Step 1 using the rocks and 4 new chalk pieces.

Put on lid!

8 rocks
4 pieces of chalk

### Materials

8 small rocks

plastic jar

8 pieces of chalk

water          timer or stopwatch

### Explain Your Results

**3.** How did the chalk change after being shaken with rocks for 1 minute? for 3 more minutes?

.................................................................................

.................................................................................

**4. Infer** Compared with shaking the chalk with only rocks, what effect did shaking with both rocks and water have on the chalk?

.................................................................................

.................................................................................

myscienceonline.com | Explore It! Animation

4.NS.8 Identify simple patterns in data and propose explanations to account for the patterns.

I will know how weathering and erosion can change the Earth's surface.

**Words to Know**

landform
weathering
erosion

## Earth's Surface

The outer surface of Earth is a layer of rock called the crust. The crust covers all of Earth. In places such as the oceans, the crust is under water.

A mountain is one of many different shapes that Earth's crust can have. Earth's surface also has many other natural features, or **landforms.** Landforms can be different sizes and shapes. Plains are flat landforms on high or low ground, and plateaus are flat landforms on high ground. Along coasts, landforms such as peninsulas extend into the water. Valleys and canyons are also landforms.

Some landforms take shape quickly, while others form over a long time. A mountain may take millions of years to form. But rocks rolling down the side of that mountain can change it in a hurry. Think of what happens to the large amounts of soil that a flood carries from one place to another.

1. **Describe** What landforms are near where you live?

..................................................

..................................................

..................................................

..................................................

..................................................

..................................................

Earth's crust is miles thick, but if Earth were the size of a peach, the crust would only be as thick as the peach's skin.

# Weathering

Earth's landforms change constantly. Rocks in Earth's crust are slowly broken into smaller pieces in a process called **weathering.** Many factors can cause weathering. There are two types of weathering, chemical weathering and physical weathering.

## Chemical Weathering

During chemical weathering, chemicals cause rocks to change into different materials and break down. For example, rainwater mixes with carbon dioxide in the air to form a weak acid. When it rains, the acid combines with the rock material to form a new chemical. The new chemical washes away, causing the rock to break down.

Animals and plants give off chemicals that can cause weathering. Sometimes the activities of people also add chemicals to the environment.

Water and warm temperatures are important for chemical weathering. Warmer areas or areas with a lot of rain have more chemical weathering than drier or colder areas.

2. **Analyze** (Circle) the evidence of weathering in this picture.

## Physical Weathering

In physical weathering, rocks are broken into smaller pieces of the same kind of rock. Water is one cause of physical weathering. Flowing water can carry particles of rock, soil, and sand. The particles scrape against larger rocks. The rocks gradually become smaller and smaller. The force of waves pounding against rocks on a shore can also cause rock to break down. Wind can also carry small particles that can weather rocks.

Ice can also cause physical weathering. Water can seep into cracks in rocks. If this water freezes, it forms ice. Ice in rock takes up more space than the water did. The ice can make the cracks in the rock deeper. The rock may eventually split.

Temperature changes to a rock's surface may also cause weathering. When a rock's surface gets hotter, it expands, or grows larger. When it gets colder, the surface contracts, or gets smaller. Some scientists think that many temperature changes can weaken the surface of rock.

Living things can cause weathering too. Plants can sprout in a crack in a rock. As these plants and their roots get bigger, they can cause the rock to split.

3. [CHALLENGE] How can water cause both chemical and physical weathering?

.........................................................................................

.........................................................................................

.........................................................................................

*Water contributed to the weathering of these rocks.*

## Erosion

Gravity, wind, water, and ice can all move pieces of weathered rock. The process of carrying away weathered bits of rock is called **erosion.**

Moving water erodes, or carries away, materials from the land. Falling rain picks up loose material from the surfaces of rocks. As the rainwater runs into streams, it takes loose, weathered material with it. Running water can carve grooves in Earth's surface that can become valleys or canyons after many years.

In colder parts of Earth, moving ice erodes landforms. Glaciers are huge sheets of ice. They have covered parts of Earth's surface for millions of years. Most glaciers move very slowly as gravity pulls them downhill. They wear away rock and soil as they move.

4. ⊙ **Draw Conclusions** What could a muddy river tell you about erosion?

.....................................................................

.....................................................................

.....................................................................

.....................................................................

## At-Home Lab

**Soil in Motion** Work with an adult. Let a hose run slowly in one spot in bare soil. Observe what happens. Let it run more quickly. How does the flow of the water affect erosion? Work with the adult to show how wind can cause erosion too.

## Deposition

As parts of Earth's surface are broken down, other parts are built up. The forces that carry away bits of weathered rock during erosion must drop them somewhere else. This laying down of pieces of rock is called deposition. Sometimes deposition happens slowly, and other times it happens very fast.

For example, waves that erode one shoreline may drop sand somewhere else to form a beach. Rivers leave material where they flow into the ocean. The deposited material from rivers forms areas called deltas. In deserts, wind drops grains of sand in mounds called sand dunes.

5. CHALLENGE Look at the photo on these pages. Based on the erosion and deposition patterns, which way do you think the river flows? Draw an arrow to indicate direction.

6. **Summarize** What is the difference between erosion and deposition?

Erosion carved this canyon along the Colorado River in Utah. The sandy area in the inner bend of the horseshoe-shaped river is deposited material.

## Gravity and Landslides

Heavy rains or earthquakes may loosen material on a steep slope. Gravity then pulls the loosened material downward. Bits of rock and soil may travel slowly downhill a little at a time. But sometimes they travel rapidly. The rapid downhill movement of a large amount of rock and soil is a landslide. Buildings, cars, trees, and other objects are sometimes carried along with the sliding soil.

Erosion and gravity can also work underground. Water underground can dissolve certain rocks, such as limestone. This can create caverns and pools underground. When these areas get too big, gravity can cause the soil above them to collapse. Sinkholes can develop rapidly or slowly.

7. ⊙ **Compare and Contrast** How is a landslide different from other kinds of erosion and deposition?

........................................................

........................................................

........................................................

........................................................

Landslide in Topanga Canyon, California

Sinkhole in Florida

myscienceonline.com | Got it? ⏱ 60-Second Video

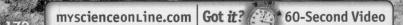

**8. Visualize** Outline the sediment that the river deposited.

Satellite images can show scientists patterns of erosion and deposition around the world.

## Studying Erosion and Deposition

Technology has improved the ways scientists can study erosion and deposition. Scientists can analyze soil to learn how erosion might affect an area. They run chemical tests and examine samples under microscopes to predict how soil might erode. For example, sandy soil will erode faster than soil that contains more clay. Satellite images can also help track erosion and deposition. By looking at photos taken from space, scientists can study how weathered rock has moved in the past. With this data, they can then predict how rock might continue to move.

**9.** [CHALLENGE] How might scientists have studied erosion and deposition before satellites were invented?

.............................................

.............................................

.............................................

## Got it?

4.2.1, 4.2.2

**10. Analyze** What is the basic difference between physical weathering and erosion?

.............................................................................................

.............................................................................................

**11. Investigate** How do microscopes and satellites help scientists study erosion?

.............................................................................................

.............................................................................................

⬛ **Stop!** I need help with .............................................

⏸ **Wait!** I have a question about .............................................

▶ **Go!** Now I know .............................................

# What are the properties of soil?

4.2.1 Demonstrate and describe how smaller rocks come from the breakage and weathering of larger rocks in a process that occurs over a long period of time.

## Envision It!

**Describe** what you notice about the soil in this picture.

## Inquiry Explore It!

### How much water can soils hold?

☑ **1.** Put each soil in a filter cup. **Measure** the mass of each filter cup with soil. Make sure they have the same mass. **Record** your **data.**

☑ **2.** Use a spoon to gently pack down the soil.

☑ **3.** Place each filter cup of soil inside a clear plastic cup. Slowly pour 50 mL of water on each soil sample. Wait 20 minutes. Record the mass of each soil sample.

| Ability of Soil to Hold Water | | |
|---|---|---|
| Type of Soil | Mass of Dry Soil (g) | Mass of Wet Soil After 20 Minutes (g) |
| Sandy soil | | |
| Clay soil | | |

### Explain Your Results

**4. Communicate** Based on your **measurements,** which type of soil holds more water? Explain.

**Materials**

water

clay soil

graduated cylinder

2 plastic cups

sandy soil    clay soil

2 filter cups

sandy soil

gram cubes

spoon

balance

clay soil

myscienceonline.com    Explore It! Animation

4.NS.5 Use measurement skills and apply appropriate units when collecting data. (Also 4.NS.8, 4.DP.9)

I will know the properties of soil, including color, texture, capacity to store water, and ability to support plant growth.

**Word to Know**
..........................................

humus

## Soil

Soil is the layer of loose material that covers most of Earth's land. A key ingredient of soil is its particles. These particles are tiny pieces of different kinds of weathered rock. Air and minerals are other nonliving ingredients in soil. These nonliving materials are important to the plants that grow in the soil.

In addition to plants, soil is full of other life. The organisms that live in soil include bacteria, fungi, worms, and insects. Some of them break down plant and animal remains. Other organisms dig in the soil. For example, prairie dogs build elaborate towns underground. Earthworms mix up the soil as they dig. This mixing improves the soil.

**1. Recognize** What are three key ingredients in soil?

.............................................................

.............................................................

**2. Analyze** How do you think soil helps prairie dogs protect themselves?

.............................................................

.............................................................

.............................................................

.............................................................

*humus*

## Properties of Soil

Soil samples from a few kilometers apart can be very different. One difference is often the amount of decayed matter in the soil. **Humus** is material in soil made up of decayed plants and animals. Humus has nutrients that plants need to grow. Other differences in soil samples have to do with the properties of the soil. These properties include the ability to support plant growth, color, texture, and the ability to hold water.

### Ability to Support Plant Growth

The three basic types of soil are sand, silt, and clay. Soil with a mixture of these three types is called loam. Loam soil has minerals, humus, air, and water that make it a good mixture for growing most plants. Loam soil holds on to water loosely enough for plant roots to bring the water into the plant. Loam soils also have nutrients that plant roots take in for the plant.

### Color

The minerals in a soil may affect its color. Iron makes soil look red. Humus may affect color too. Soil with a lot of humus is a dark brown color.

### Texture

The texture, or feel, of soil can depend on the size of the particles in the soil. Large particles feel rough. Small particles feel smooth.

3. **Generalize** How does particle size affect the texture of a soil?

..................................................................................................

..................................................................................................

..................................................................................................

## At-Home Lab

**Your State Crop**
Find information about a major crop grown in your state. What type of soil does your state crop need? How much water does it need? Share your information with the class.

THE BIG I Will Know...

## Ability to Hold Water

The size of the particles in soil can affect how well the soil holds water. Large particles have many spaces between them, so water easily passes through this soil. Medium-sized particles are closer together and hold water well. Water passes slowly through small particles.

| Type of Soil | Color | Texture | Ability to Hold Water |
|---|---|---|---|
| Sand | Sand can be different colors, such as tan, white, green, and black. | Sandy soil feels rough and gritty. | Water passes through the large particles of sand quickly. |
| Silt | Silt is usually different shades of brown, depending on the materials that are in it. | Silt feels smoother than sand particles. | The medium-sized particles of silt hold water well. |
| Clay | The colors of clay include red, grey, and blue. | Wet clay feels smooth and sticky. | The small clay particles absorb water and hold tightly together. |

4. ◉ **Draw Conclusions** What might you conclude about soil that is very dark brown in color?

........................................

........................................

........................................

5. **Infer** Which type of soil is most likely to flood during a heavy rain storm? Explain.

........................................

........................................

........................................

........................................

........................................

*This beach is made up of sand. Volcanic rock makes the sand look black.*

Do the math!

## Read a Circle Graph

Loam is a mixture of sand, silt, and clay. It also contains humus, which has many minerals and other nutrients. Water and air are in loam too. The graph shows the amount of each ingredient in one sample of loam.

Sand, Silt, and Clay 45%

Humus

Water 25%

Air 25%

**1** What percentage of this sample is humus?

........................................................................

**2** What are possible percentages of sand, silt, and clay in this soil?
   A. 9%, 10%, 25%
   B. 11%, 15%, 19%
   C. 18%, 17%, 6%
   D. 19%, 16%, 12%

**3** What percentage of this sample is rock particles and once-living material?

........................................................................

**4** **Predict** How well do you think loam holds water? Explain.

........................................................................

........................................................................

........................................................................

myscienceonline.com | Got it? 60-Second Video

## Crop Growth

Crops are plants that farmers grow for food. Crops grow best in soil that has many nutrients. Different crops use different nutrients. If the soil has too much sand or clay, the crops cannot soak up the nutrients.

Good farming can replace nutrients in soil naturally. Farmers can plant certain crops that put nutrients back into the soil. Crops that are plowed under also add nutrients to the soil.

6. **CHALLENGE** Why might farmers plant their crops in one field one year, and plant them in a different field the next year?

......................................................................

......................................................................

......................................................................

......................................................................

*Like all crops, these crops need nutrient-rich soil to grow. Nutrients that most plants need include nitrogen and phosphorus.*

## Got it?

4.2.1

7. **Recognize** What are the properties of soil?

......................................................................

......................................................................

8. **Predict** Suppose the organisms that break down plant and animal remains were removed from soil. What would happen to the properties of the soil?

......................................................................

......................................................................

**Stop!** I need help with ....................................................

**Wait!** I have a question about ......................................

**Go!** Now I know ....................................................

# How does Earth's surface change rapidly?

🔵 **4.2.3** Demonstrate and describe how earthquakes, volcanoes, and landslides suddenly change the shape of the land.

## Envision It!

How is the shape of the land changing?

## my planet diary

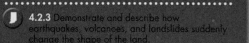

Most earthquakes occur at points where two plates, or two large pieces of Earth's surface, meet. But faults, or cracks in rock where Earth's crust can move, can form anywhere in Earth's crust and mantle. The Wabash Valley Fault System is a series of underground faults along the southern border of Illinois and Indiana. Movement along the faults caused medium-sized earthquakes in 1968, 2002, and 2008. The 2008 earthquake was felt in 16 states and in places more than 720 kilometers away.

Scientists cannot predict earthquakes. However, they can study patterns in Earth's crust to try to find out where earthquakes have occurred and how severe they were. By examining Earth's crust, scientists found evidence that the region has had earthquakes for at least 20,000 years.

How might people in the Wabash Valley Fault System prepare for earthquakes?

.................................................

.................................................

.................................................

.................................................

.................................................

.................................................

The Rapp-Owen Granary in New Hope, Indiana, contains a seismograph to measure earthquakes.

I will know how earthquakes, volcanoes, and landslides can suddenly change the shape of the land.

**Words to Know**

fault          epicenter
focus          volcano

## Earth's Moving Plates

Earth's outer crust rests on top of another layer called the mantle. The crust and the top of the mantle, together, are divided into very large pieces called plates. The plates move all the time. This movement can cause rapid changes in Earth's surface. Volcanoes and earthquakes often occur along or near places where the plates come together.

Look at the picture. It shows an area in Iceland where two plates are moving away from each other. The land on the left is part of the North American plate. This is the same plate that most of the United States is on. The land on the right is part of the plate that much of Europe and Asia are on. Iceland has many volcanoes and earthquakes because it is atop these two plates.

1. **Recognize** Why does Iceland have many volcanoes and earthquakes?

........................................................

........................................................

........................................................

........................................................

........................................................

........................................................

## Earthquakes

Earthquakes happen along faults. A **fault** is a break or crack in rocks where Earth's crust can move suddenly. Faults can form anywhere in Earth's crust or mantle. Earthquakes most often occur at faults at or near the boundaries between Earth's plates. Sometimes rocks along a fault get stuck. The plates continue their slow movement, which puts stress on the rocks. Then the plates move suddenly.

### Slipping plates

This sudden plate movement gives off a large amount of energy. Some of the energy travels in vibrations, or waves. These waves cause the shaking of an earthquake. Plate movements often happen far underground. The place where plates start to slip is called the **focus.** The point on Earth's surface that is directly above the focus of an earthquake is called the **epicenter.** Waves from an earthquake travel in all directions underground. Because of this, people far away may feel an earthquake, but the damage it causes is usually greatest near the epicenter.

2. **Demonstrate** Circle the area where the most damage would occur from the earthquake.

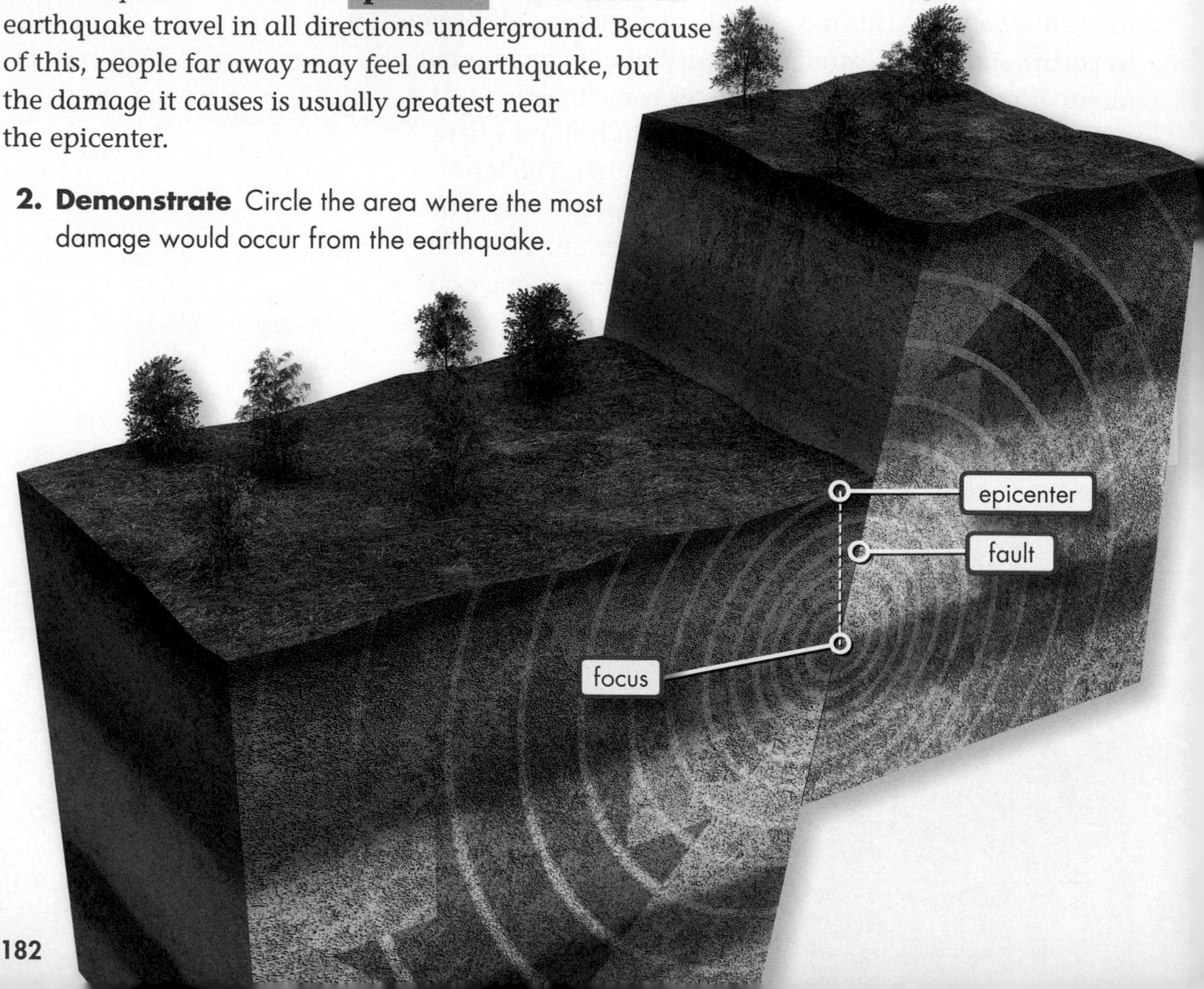

epicenter

fault

focus

### Measuring earthquakes

Scientists use tools called seismographs to locate and measure earthquakes. Seismographs have parts that are attached to Earth's crust. These parts detect vibrations. Other parts of a seismograph move freely and record the vibrations. More than 200,000 earthquakes around the world are located each year. Scientists estimate that there are actually several million earthquakes each year! Most of these are too small to be measured or felt.

A few earthquakes are powerful enough to damage buildings, roads, and bridges. Sometimes earthquakes can break gas or water pipes underground. This can lead to flooding or fires. In 1906 and 1989, strong earthquakes broke gas lines in San Francisco. The broken gas lines in 1906 caused fires that burned for three days and destroyed 500 city blocks.

Seismograms are used to measure and locate earthquakes.

3. **Analyze** Suppose scientists develop better measuring tools. The new tools are able to locate twice as many earthquakes per year. Does that mean the number of earthquakes is increasing? Why or why not?

....................................................................

....................................................................

An earthquake in Kobe, Japan in 1995 collapsed this railway.

## Lightning Lab

**Earthquake Model**
Create a hill of soil or sand in a pan. Give the pan a quick shake. How does the movement affect the hill?

183

## Volcanoes

Sometimes molten rock, or lava, comes out of Earth's surface. A **volcano** is an opening in Earth's crust where gases, ash, and molten rock can reach the surface. A volcano can take many years to form. However, a volcanic eruption can change Earth's surface quickly. Most volcanoes form underwater where two plates pull apart. However, volcanoes on land often form at areas where two plates meet and one slides underneath the other.

### How volcanoes form

Earth's mantle is almost entirely solid. But when one plate moves below another plate, it brings down water that helps the rock partially melt. The rock becomes a hot liquid material called magma. Magma is lighter than solid rock, so it quickly rises upward. When a volcano erupts, the magma reaches the surface and is called lava.

4. **Identify** Find and label another possible vent on this volcano.

5. ◉ **Draw Conclusions** Select three facts from the text above. Then draw a conclusion.

Layers of cooled rock from eruptions can form a cone shape around a volcano.

A spot from which lava erupts is called a vent.

**Facts**                    **Conclusion**

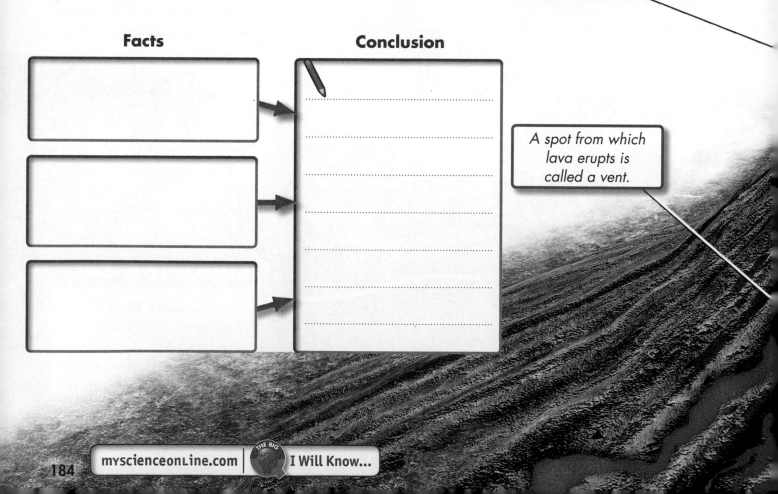

mYscienceonLine.com | I Will Know...

## Effects of volcanoes

Volcanoes can form on continents. They can also build from the ocean floor. A volcanic island forms when a volcano reaches the surface of the water. The state of Hawaii is a string of islands formed in this way.

Volcanoes can do more than ooze fountains of lava. Gases, such as water vapor and carbon dioxide, are often mixed with the lava. Trapped gases can have enough pressure to blow apart the side of a volcano during an eruption. These trapped gases can push lava high into the air. While it is still in the air, this lava may cool into ash or rocks. However, not all volcanic eruptions are violent.

Volcanic eruptions can also affect the climate. In 1991, Mount Pinatubo in the Philippines erupted. It sent huge amounts of ash and other particles into the atmosphere. These particles reduced the amount of sunlight that reached Earth. As a result, average temperatures were cooler around the world by as much as one degree for more than a year.

6. **◉ Cause and Effect**
Draw an example of how Mount Pinatubo's eruption might have reduced temperatures.

*A bowl-shaped area, or crater, may form around the main vent.*

# Tsunamis and Landslides

Earthquakes and volcanoes can change Earth's surface on their own. However, the energy released by an earthquake or volcanic eruption can cause more events, such as tsunamis and landslides.

## Tsunamis

An earthquake or eruption under the ocean can cause a series of huge waves of water called a tsunami. The waves in a tsunami can start out small. They may only be a few inches high. Tsunami waves get higher as they get closer to the shore. The highest tsunami ever recorded struck Lituya Bay, Alaska, in 1958. Its waves reached 520 meters up the sides of a nearby mountain.

A tsunami may crash into a coast like a wall of water. It may also appear like a series of high, fast-moving tides which flood the coast. The water can reach several kilometers inland. Tsunamis can destroy structures and wash away soil. In 2004 an earthquake under the ocean near Sumatra, Indonesia caused tsunamis that affected at least eleven countries.

**7. ⊙ Cause and Effect**
Study the photo on this page. How do you think the boat might have ended up where it did?

...................................................

...................................................

...................................................

effects of a tsunami in India

myscienceonLine.com | Got it? | 60-Second Video

## Landslides

A landslide is a rapid downhill movement of a large amount of rock and soil. Energy from earthquakes and volcanic eruptions can cause landslides. Heavy rains can increase the risk of landslides. So can human activity, such as mining or construction. Landslides can happen on continents and underwater. Tsunamis may also occur as a result of an underwater landslide.

8. **Demonstrate** Draw how an underwater landslide may cause a tsunami.

Erosion, gravity, rainfall, human activity, and energy from earthquakes and volcanoes can all cause landslides.

## Got it?

🔊 4.2.2, 4.2.3

9. **Describe** How can earthquakes, volcanoes, and landslides suddenly change Earth's surface?

..................................................................................................

..................................................................................................

10. **Describe** Why could the damage from an earthquake be greatest at the epicenter?

..................................................................................................

..................................................................................................

⬜ **Stop!** I need help with ........................................................

⏸ **Wait!** I have a question about ...........................................

▶ **Go!** Now I know ....................................................................

## Lesson 4

# How do people change Earth's surface?

**4.2.6** Describe ways in which humans have changed the natural environment that have been detrimental or beneficial.

## Envision It!

**Tell** one way human activity has affected this environment.

---

## Inquiry Explore It!

### How can pollution affect water?

People and other living things affect the environment. In this activity, you observe "water pollution" and infer how it could affect water plants.

☑ **1.** Shine a flashlight through a cup of water.
**Observe** how clear the water is.
Observe how much light shines out the other side.

☑ **2.** Add 10 drops of milk. Stir with a spoon.
Repeat Step 1.

### Materials

plastic cup of water

milk

dropper

spoon

flashlight

### Explain Your Results

**3. Draw a Conclusion** How did the milk affect the amount of light that traveled all the way through the water and out the side of the cup?

.............................................................

**4. Infer** How might cloudy water caused by pollution affect plants that grow in lakes or rivers?

.............................................................

.............................................................

myscienceonline.com | **Explore It!** Animation

**4.NS.8** Identify simple patterns in data and propose explanations to account for the patterns. (Also **4.NS.3**)

I will know some positive and negative ways in which humans impact the environment.

**Words to Know**

pollution
reclamation

## People and the Environment

Like all living things, people interact with their environment, or all the living and nonliving things around them. We get our food, shelter, and water from the land and organisms around us. Unlike other organisms, we can change large parts of the environment to meet our needs. We cut down trees to provide us with lumber and land for houses. We clear prairies to plant crops or build roads. When we change the environment, however, we sometimes upset the balance in the environment.

1. **Analyze** Study the photo. How have humans changed this environment to meet their needs? How might this change affect other organisms?

..................................................................

..................................................................

..................................................................

*People changed this area when they built a road.*

## Pollution

As humans, we use resources and energy to meet our needs. As we use products, we create waste. The waste from products made or used by people is called **pollution.** Pollution can affect the air, water, and land.

### Air Pollution

Many of the things we do release dust, dirt, and harmful gases into the air. Automobiles and factories can release chemicals into the air. These chemicals can be dangerous to breathe. The chemicals can also harm plants. Animals that depend on these plants may lose their source of food or shelter.

### Water Pollution

Wastes and chemicals can get into rivers, lakes, and the ocean. Water then becomes polluted. Some of these substances enter the water through sewer systems. Others mix with water vapor in the air and return to Earth in rainwater. Still other chemicals are used on land to help plants grow or to kill insects. Rain washes these chemicals off the land and into the water. Some of these chemicals can harm or kill fish and other organisms that live in or near the water. Some of the pollutants in rivers and streams may end up in Earth's ocean. Sometimes spills and leaks occur during the drilling and shipping of oil. Then, oil becomes a pollutant that can harm plants and animals. Algae, plants, mollusks, and fish become coated with oil and may die. Birds that are coated with oil often drown.

2. ◎ **Main Idea and Details** (Circle) the main ideas on this page. Study the photos. How do the photos provide details to support the main idea?

..................................................

..................................................

Factories make products people need but can also release chemicals into the air.

Oil from a spill off the coast of Alaska coats this bird.

## Land Pollution

Garbage, litter, and other substances can pollute the land. Humans produce huge amounts of garbage. The average person throws away about two kilograms of garbage each day. Most of this trash is dumped into areas called landfills and then covered with soil.

Disposing of hazardous wastes can cause other kinds of land pollution. Hazardous wastes are substances that are very harmful to humans and other organisms. These substances may be poisonous, cause disease, start fires, or react dangerously with other substances. Until recently, most hazardous wastes were put into containers and buried in the ground. Some of these containers leaked. The hazardous wastes seeped into the ground or water and damaged nearby environments.

### Controlling land pollution

Most trash today is dumped into areas called landfills. Modern landfills are designed to protect underground water sources and control pollution. Landfills have liners made of clay or plastic to protect the ground below. Garbage added to a landfill is then covered with soil to keep it away from air and water. When landfills are out of space, they are closed and watched carefully. Land above a closed landfill is often used for parks or to construct new buildings.

3. **Evaluate** Tell how air and land pollution can also cause water pollution.

### Go Green

**Talking Trash**
Observe the amount of trash your family generates in a week. What activities generate the most trash? How could those activities generate less trash?

After this landfill was closed, scientists designed a way to use the gas from the rotting garbage for energy.

## Stripping Away the Land

Many valuable substances lie under Earth's surface. One of these substances is coal. Strip mining is one way to get coal that is below Earth's surface. Huge machines dig up and clear away the top layers of soil. Large holes are left. The land surrounding the holes may then erode. Piles of soil and rock can wash into ponds and rivers and affect nearby environments. Another way of mining involves digging deep, narrow tunnels, called shafts, underground. Abandoned underground mines can be dangerous. When underground mines collapse, they can cause damage on the surface.

Restoring the land is important for the environment. When the land is restored, animals can return to the area. If the land cannot be restored, crops are planted so that the land is used for other purposes.

4. **Analyze** How does mining help humans? How can it hurt?

.......................................................................................

.......................................................................................

.......................................................................................

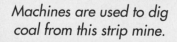

Machines are used to dig coal from this strip mine.

## Land Reclamation

Coal mining in some states began in the 1840s. For more than 100 years, no repairs were made to lands that had been strip-mined. Beginning in the 1970s, laws were passed to regulate strip mining.

Federal law now requires that land disturbed by mining must be reclaimed. **Reclamation** is the process of restoring land after it has been used. In mining reclamation, mining companies must replace rock and soil that were removed. They must replant the area with crops or native trees and grasses. Mining companies need to submit plans to reclaim the land they use before they begin mining. For example, mining companies must study the ecosystems before any digging begins. These studies include how a mine would affect nearby fish and wildlife, as well as the land.

Indiana is one state that has reclaimed some mining areas. Coal mines in southwestern Indiana have been restored to farmland and forests. An abandoned mine in Turkey Run State Park was turned into a habitat for the endangered Indiana Bat.

*Bat habitat in Indiana's Turkey Run State Park*

5. ◎ **Draw Conclusions** Tell what conclusion you might draw about the number of mines that have been reclaimed.

*These cattle are grazing on a former strip mine in Wyoming.*

# Preserving the Environment

Our nation has many natural treasures. You can watch millions of gallons of water cascade over Niagara Falls. You can look out over the breathtaking Grand Canyon. The United States has established the National Park Service to preserve nature's beauty, historic sites, and the environments of many plants and animals.

## Yellowstone National Park

In 1872, Yellowstone became the world's first national park. Most of the park is in Wyoming. Many kinds of trees and other plants and animals, such as bears and moose, live there. Yellowstone's most unusual features are bubbling mud pots and geysers that shoot boiling water high into the air.

Yellowstone National Park

## Saguaro National Park

Saguaro National Park, in Arizona, is in the Sonoran Desert. The Sonoran Desert is home to more species of plants and animals than any other American desert. It is the only region in the world where giant saguaro cactuses grow. This monument preserves ancient villages as well as modern wildlife.

## Okefenokee National Wildlife Refuge

This refuge in Georgia is the home of many plants and animals. Cranes, herons, egrets, and other waterfowl wade in the marshy areas. Bobcats, deer, otters, and other animals roam in the grassy areas. They are protected from poachers, people who hunt without a license. Decaying vegetation sometimes makes the water in the Okefenokee brown.

Saguaro National Park

6. **Summarize** What is one way animals are protected in national parks?

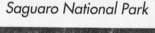

Okefenokee National Wildlife Refuge

myscienceonline.com | Got it? 🕐 60-Second Video

## Private Conservation

Private groups and businesses are also looking for ways to balance people and the environment. Some companies set aside land as wildlife preservation areas. Land trusts are private organizations that work to preserve environments. Areas preserved by land trusts may be available for use by people, or they may be for wildlife only.

**7. Describe** Research a national park, state park, or private wildlife area near where you live. Write the name of it here. Tell a partner what you learned.

........................................................................................

*Barters Island in Maine is part of the Boothbay Region Land Trust.*

## Got it?

○ 4.2.6

**8. Describe** What are some ways in which people change the natural environment?

........................................................................................

........................................................................................

**9. Summarize** What are some of the things people do to protect the natural environment?

........................................................................................

........................................................................................

 **Stop!** I need help with ........................................................

**Wait!** I have a question about ................................................

**Go!** Now I know ....................................................................

mysciencEonLine.com | **Got it? Quiz**    195

# What are natural resources?

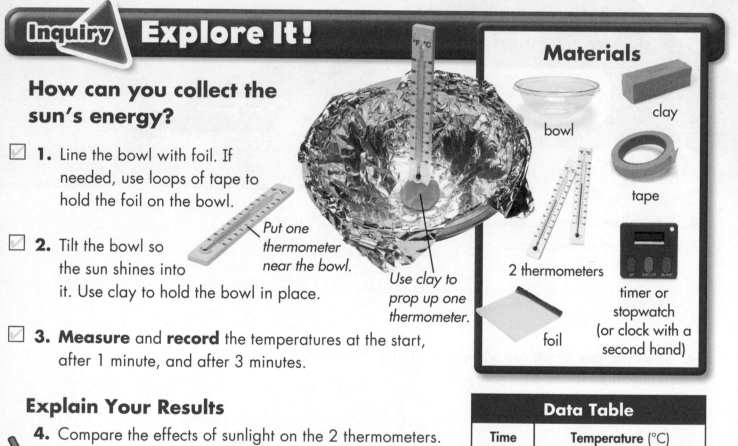

## Envision It!

4.2.4 Investigate earth materials that serve as natural resources and gather data to determine which are in limited supply.
4.2.5 Describe methods that humans currently use to extend the use of natural resources.

**Tell** what resources are available in this picture.

## Inquiry Explore It!

### How can you collect the sun's energy?

☑ **1.** Line the bowl with foil. If needed, use loops of tape to hold the foil on the bowl.

*Put one thermometer near the bowl.*

☑ **2.** Tilt the bowl so the sun shines into it. Use clay to hold the bowl in place.

*Use clay to prop up one thermometer.*

☑ **3. Measure** and **record** the temperatures at the start, after 1 minute, and after 3 minutes.

### Materials

bowl

clay

tape

2 thermometers

foil

timer or stopwatch (or clock with a second hand)

### Explain Your Results

**4.** Compare the effects of sunlight on the 2 thermometers.

**5. Infer** What made the temperatures different?

| Data Table | | |
|---|---|---|
| **Time** | **Temperature (°C)** | |
| | **Near Bowl** | **In Bowl** |
| **At start** | | |
| **After 1 min** | | |
| **After 3 min** | | |

4.1.1 Describe and investigate the different ways in which heat can be generated. 4.NS.8 Identify simple patterns in data and propose explanations to account for the patterns. (Also 4.1.2, 4.DP.9)

I will know that people need resources and that some resources can be replaced in nature and some cannot.

## Words to Know

renewable resource
nonrenewable resource

## Natural Resources

Are you wearing jeans? Are you holding a pencil? Did you drink some water today? You're using natural resources! Natural resources are supplies found in nature. Plants and animals are natural resources. So are nonliving things such as air, water, soil, minerals, and sunlight.

All living things depend on natural resources. Plants need air, sunlight, soil, and water to live. People need air and water too. They use plant and animal resources for food. Earth's resources also provide the raw materials and energy that we use to make the products we need. Everything we eat, use, or buy has been made from or is a natural resource.

| Products Consumed per Person in 2005 | | |
|---|---|---|
| | **Gasoline** (L) | **Paper products** (kg) |
| The average person in the world used... | 186.9 | 55.83 |
| The average person in the U.S. used... | 1,772.6 | 302.97 |
| This country used the most per person: | United States 1,772.6 | Luxembourg 340.16 |

Sources: U.S. Energy Information Administration;
Food & Agriculture Organization of the United Nations

1. **Apply** Look around your classroom. What resources do you need during the school day?

2. **Analyze** What natural resources are used to create the products listed in the chart?

myscienceonline.com | Envision It!  197

## Renewable Resources

Earth has two types of natural resources, renewable and nonrenewable. **Renewable resources** are resources that can be replaced. Plants and animals are examples of renewable resources. So is the oxygen in the air we breathe. These resources are renewable as long as they are replaced as fast as they are used.

### Water

Water is one of our most important renewable resources. All living things need water to survive. Humans also use water for things such as cooking and bathing.

Earth constantly recycles its water through precipitation and evaporation. This makes water a renewable resource. But only one percent of Earth's water is drinkable. The rest is either salt water in the oceans or frozen in glaciers and polar ice caps. Also, not all people live near water sources. Gathering drinkable water and keeping it safe for people to use takes time and more resources.

3. ◎ **Draw Conclusions**
What conclusions might you draw about the amount of drinkable water on Earth?

.................................................................

.................................................................

.................................................................

.................................................................

.................................................................

.................................................................

## Solar and Wind Energy

People use energy to run machines, heat and cool homes, and help grow food. Solar energy is a renewable resource. Energy from the sun can be used to heat buildings. Solar cells can change energy from the sun into electrical energy.

Wind is another source of renewable energy. Windmills can be used to run machinery and to produce electricity.

Solar and wind energy do not cause pollution. Sunlight will not run out for billions of years. But neither solar nor wind energy is available all the time. Some people think windmills are noisy or ugly. Systems to collect solar energy are expensive to make. Factories that make certain kinds of solar cells also produce dangerous wastes.

4. **Identify Underline** the advantages of renewable energy. **Circle** the disadvantages of renewable energy.

## Do the math!

### Read a Circle Graph

The circle graph shows how an average family of four in the United States uses water each day. The average household uses about 1,049 liters of water per day.

**Daily Water Use, Family of Four**

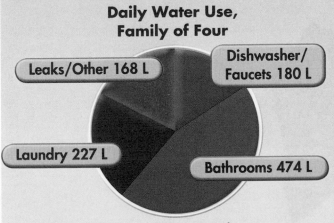

Leaks/Other 168 L

Dishwasher/Faucets 180 L

Laundry 227 L

Bathrooms 474 L

*Source: American Water Works Association*

**1** How much water does the average U.S. family use in bathrooms each week?
A. 3,318 L
B. 1,176 L
C. 7,343 L
D. 1,260 L

**2** In a family of four, about how much water does each person use per day?
A. 4,196 L
B. 2,620 L
C. 262 L
D. 26.2 L

# Nonrenewable Resources

All minerals are nonrenewable resources. **Nonrenewable resources** are resources that exist in limited amounts or are used faster than they can be replaced in nature. People use minerals and other nonrenewable resources to make products and to provide energy.

## Fossil Fuels

Oil is the common name for petroleum. Oil and coal are nonrenewable resources. They are fuels, which means that they are burned to provide energy. Oil is also used to make various products.

Coal and oil are called fossil fuels because they were made from organisms that lived long ago. After the organisms died, their remains and the unused stored energy stored in them became buried under layers of sediments. Over millions of years, pressure, heat, and decaying action changed the remains into coal, oil, and natural gas.

## Ores

Mineral resources are often found in ores. An ore is a rock that is rich in valuable minerals. Fossil fuels and ores are removed from below Earth's surface. But ores are removed for the minerals they contain, not for burning as fuel.

People use mineral resources in different ways. For example, iron ore contains the metal iron. Often the iron is mixed with other materials to make steel. Steel is used to make things ranging from skyscrapers to paper clips.

*Oil and gas drilling platform*

5. ◉ **Compare and Contrast** How are ores and fossil fuels alike? How are they different?

..............................................................

..............................................................

..............................................................

..............................................................

..............................................................

..............................................................

..............................................................

*iron ore*

myscienceonline.com | **Got it?** 🕐 **60-Second Video**

## How Resources Can Last Longer

People use natural resources to make products they use in their daily lives. As people use more and more resources, fewer nonrenewable resources will be available in the future. Conservation means using what you need as efficiently as possible. You can reduce unnecessary resource use in many ways. For example, to travel short distances, you can walk or ride a bike. You can drink from a reusable container instead of buying bottled water and throwing the bottle away.

Recycling is saving or using materials again instead of treating them as waste. Some products and materials are easier to recycle than others.

6. **Apply** Think about the resources you used today. How might you conserve them in the future?

..............................................................................................................

..............................................................................................................

 **4.2.4, 4.2.5**

7. **Analyze** How might nonrenewable resources be spent to collect renewable resources?

..............................................................................................................

..............................................................................................................

8. **UNLOCK THE BIG** Think about what you learned in this lesson. How do Earth's resources change?

..............................................................................................................

..............................................................................................................

⬛ **Stop!** I need help with ............................................................................

⏸ **Wait!** I have a question about ..............................................................

▶ **Go!** Now I know ......................................................................................

## Why are earth materials important?

Earth materials, such as rocks and minerals, are natural resources used to help create many different products for people.

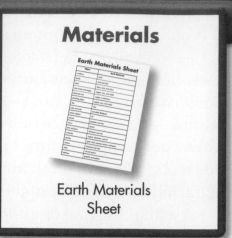

**Materials**

Earth Materials Sheet

### Follow a Procedure

☑ **1. Collect Data** Work in groups. Use the Earth Materials Sheet. Identify 3 classroom objects. List the earth materials used to help make these objects.

> **Inquiry Skill** Recording data on a chart can help you make **inferences.**

| Objects Found in the Classroom | |
|---|---|
| **Classroom Object** | **Earth Materials** |
| | |
| | |
| | |

☑ **2.** Take an earth materials walk around your school.

☑ **3.** Identify at least 9 objects that are made from earth materials. **Record** them on your chart.

4.2.4 Investigate earth materials that serve as natural resources and gather data to determine which are in limited supply. (Also **4.NS.3, 4.NS.7**)

| Objects Found in the Earth Materials Walk | | |
|---|---|---|
| | Object | Earth Materials |
| Building materials | | |
| Everyday items | | |
| Consumable items | | |
| Jewelry | | |
| Decorations | | |

## Analyze and Conclude

4. **UNLOCK THE BIG Q** **Infer** Using your **data,** which earth materials are being used the most? Why is this important?

..............................................................................................................

..............................................................................................................

..............................................................................................................

# The Galápagos Islands

**4.2.3**

The Galápagos Islands are a chain of islands located in the Pacific Ocean. This chain of islands is about 1,000 kilometers (600 miles) west of Ecuador, a country in South America. The chain has more than 100 islands in all. Some of the major islands have their own names.

The Galápagos Islands have not always existed. They were formed by volcanoes and are probably no more than five million years old.

How do volcanoes form islands? Volcanoes can erupt underwater as well as on land. Each time volcanoes erupt, more lava builds up. Eventually, volcanoes can build up above the surface of the ocean and form volcanic islands such as the islands that make up the Galápagos Islands.

Galápagos Islands

*Galápagos* means tortoises in Spanish.
Why might these islands have been named the Galápagos?

.................................................................................................

.................................................................................................

# Vocabulary Smart Cards

landform
weathering
erosion
humus
fault
focus
epicenter
volcano
pollution
reclamation
renewable resource
nonrenewable
  resource

## Play a Game!

Work with a partner.
Your partner chooses a
Vocabulary Smart Card
term. Hold up the card with
the word side facing your
partner. Ask your partner to
use the term in a sentence.
Provide the definition if
necessary.

Have your partner repeat
with another Vocabulary
Smart Card.

**humus**

humus

**landform**

accidente
geográfico

**fault**

fault

falla

**weathering**

meteorización

**focus**

focus

foco

**erosion**

erosión

natural land feature on Earth's surface

Draw an example.

formación natural en la superficie terrestre

a material in soil made up of decayed plants and animals

Write a sentence using this word.

.................................................

.................................................

material que se encuentra en el suelo y está formado por plantas y animales descompuestos

mountain

canyon  landform

volcano

## Make a Word Wheel!

Choose a vocabulary term and write it in the center of the Word Wheel graphic organizer. Write synonyms or related words on the wheel spokes.

process of rocks in Earth's crust slowly being broken into smaller pieces

Write a sentence using the verb form of this word.

.................................................

.................................................

proceso de las rocas de la corteza terrestre que se van rompiendo en trozos más pequeños

break or crack in rocks where Earth's crust can move suddenly

Write a sentence using this word.

.................................................

.................................................

fisura o grieta en las rocas donde la corteza terrestre puede desplazarse en forma repentina

process of carrying away weathered bits of rock

Draw an example.

proceso por el cual se mueven pedacitos de roca desgastada

place where plates start to slip

Write a sentence using this word.

.................................................

.................................................

.................................................

lugar donde las placas comienzan a deslizarse

**reclamation**

recuperación

**epicenter**

epicenter

epicentro

**renewable resource**

recurso renovable

**volcano**

volcán

**nonrenewable resource**

recurso no renovable

**pollution**

contaminación

point on Earth's surface that is directly above the focus of an earthquake

Write a sentence using this word.

........................................

........................................

........................................

punto de la superficie de la Tierra directamente sobre el foco de un terremoto

---

process of restoring land after it has been used

What is the verb form of this word?

........................................

........................................

........................................

proceso en el cual se restaura la tierra después de que ha sido utilizada

---

opening in Earth's crust where gases, ash, and molten rock can reach the surface

Draw an example.

abertura de la corteza terrestre por el cual gases, cenizas y roca fundidas pueden alcanzar la superficie

---

resource that can be replaced

Write an example.

........................................

........................................

........................................

........................................

recurso que se puede reemplazar

---

waste from products made or used by people

Give three examples of this word.

........................................

........................................

........................................

desecho de los productos creados o usados por la gente

---

resource that exists in limited amounts or is used faster than it can be replaced in nature

What is the prefix of this word?

........................................

recurso que existe en cantidades limitadas o que se usa más rápido de lo que le toma a la naturaleza reponerlo

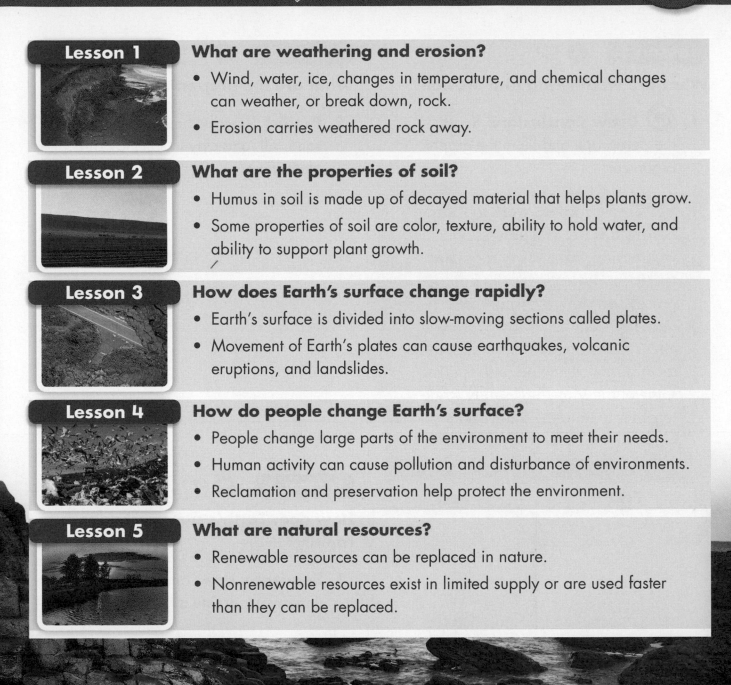

**Lesson 1**

### What are weathering and erosion?

- Wind, water, ice, changes in temperature, and chemical changes can weather, or break down, rock.
- Erosion carries weathered rock away.

**Lesson 2**

### What are the properties of soil?

- Humus in soil is made up of decayed material that helps plants grow.
- Some properties of soil are color, texture, ability to hold water, and ability to support plant growth.

**Lesson 3**

### How does Earth's surface change rapidly?

- Earth's surface is divided into slow-moving sections called plates.
- Movement of Earth's plates can cause earthquakes, volcanic eruptions, and landslides.

**Lesson 4**

### How do people change Earth's surface?

- People change large parts of the environment to meet their needs.
- Human activity can cause pollution and disturbance of environments.
- Reclamation and preservation help protect the environment.

**Lesson 5**

### What are natural resources?

- Renewable resources can be replaced in nature.
- Nonrenewable resources exist in limited supply or are used faster than they can be replaced.

# Chapter Review

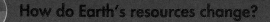

How do Earth's resources change?

**Lesson 1**  4.2.1

**What are weathering and erosion?**

1. ⊙ **Draw Conclusions** Read the paragraph and fill in the graphic organizer.

> Several processes work to shape Earth's surface. The process of weathering wears away rocks and particles. However, during another process, erosion, the weathered material is moved away. Various forces move the weathered material, including water, wind, and ice. Yet some of the same forces may work together to drop the rocks and particles in a new location. This process is called deposition.

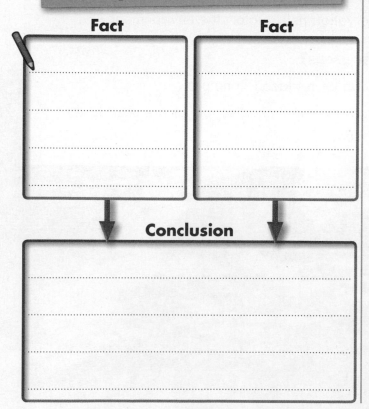

Fact

Fact

Conclusion

**Lesson 2**  4.2.1

**What are the properties of soil?**

2. **Predict** Describe how the amounts of sand, silt, and clay in soil may affect plant growth.

.................................................................

.................................................................

.................................................................

.................................................................

.................................................................

.................................................................

.................................................................

**Lesson 3**  4.2.3

**How does Earth's surface change rapidly?**

3. **Sequence** How can volcanic activity underwater create a tsunami?

.................................................................

.................................................................

.................................................................

.................................................................

.................................................................

.................................................................

.................................................................

.................................................................

## Lesson 4    4.2.6

### How do people change Earth's surface?

**4. Vocabulary** Restoring land from unused mines is called
- A. reclamation.
- B. recycling.
- C. preservation.
- D. pollution.

**5. Cause and Effect** How might air pollution harm an organism's source of food?

........................................................

........................................................

........................................................

........................................................

........................................................

**6. Analyze** List one way in which the National Park Service benefits humans, and one way it benefits other organisms.

........................................................

........................................................

........................................................

........................................................

## Lesson 5    4.2.4, 4.2.5

### What are natural resources?

**7. Classify** (Circle) the resources in this list that are renewable.

petroleum

solar energy

soil

water

wind

minerals

silicon

**8.**  **How do Earth's resources change?**

Think of a rocky cliff on a beach. What natural forces have shaped this landform? What forces continue to change it?

........................................................

........................................................

........................................................

........................................................

........................................................

## Multiple Choice

**1** Which of these is probably the result of erosion caused by flowing water?

    A. a mountain

    B. a canyon

    C. a glacier

    D. a sand dune

                   4.2.2

## Constructed Response

**2** Look at this symbol.

What is the purpose of this symbol? On what items might you find it?

.................................................................

.................................................................

.................................................................

.................................................................

.................................................................

.................................................................

                   4.2.5

## Extended Response

**3** This diagram shows the interior of a volcano.

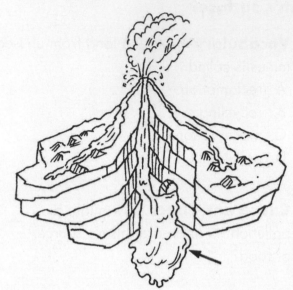

What does the arrow point to?

.................................................................

.................................................................

How can an erupting volcano change Earth's surface?

.................................................................

.................................................................

.................................................................

How can an erupting volcano affect the air?

.................................................................

.................................................................

                   4.2.3

🕐 4.2.5

# Car Engineer

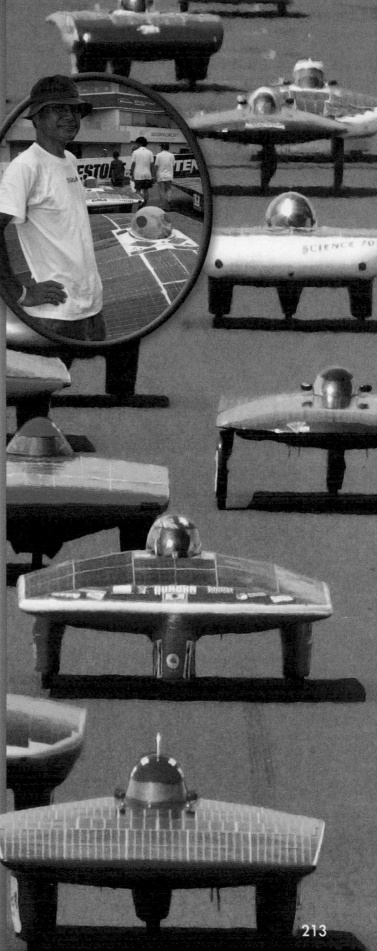

Would you like to build a car that uses renewable resources? You could become part of a team designing solar-powered cars. The North American Solar Challenge is a solar car competition. Students from colleges and universities in the United States and Canada design solar-powered cars and race them across the country.

The students work in teams. The teams put their cars through tests and inspections to be sure they are safe. Then the race is on!

The solar cars are flashy, but they have some advantages and disadvantages. They seat only one or two people. There is not much space to carry things, and as you may have guessed, they run only during the day! Even so, solar cars help us learn more about solar energy and how it can be used.

Most of the students who build the cars are mainly studying science, math, and engineering. Many will become mechanical engineers and design other kinds of cars or find other ways to use solar energy.

How might creating solar cars affect Earth's other resources?

## Materials

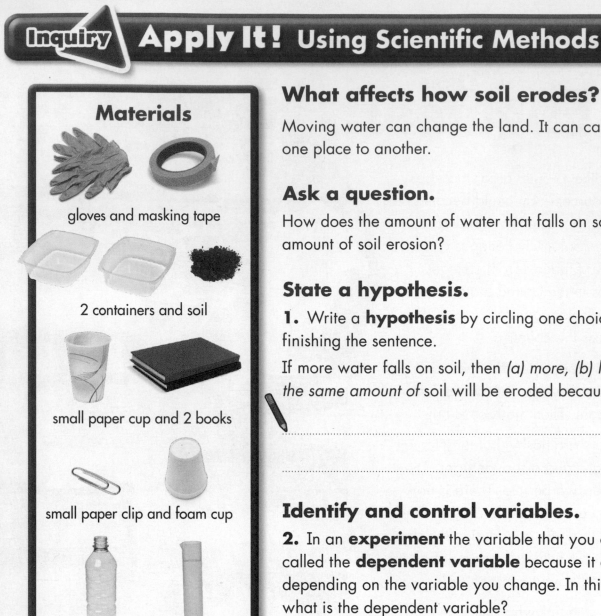

gloves and masking tape

2 containers and soil

small paper cup and 2 books

small paper clip and foam cup

water

graduated cylinder (or measuring cup)

metric ruler

### Inquiry Skill

A **hypothesis** is a statement that explains an observation. It can be tested by an experiment.

## What affects how soil erodes?

Moving water can change the land. It can carry soil from one place to another.

## Ask a question.

How does the amount of water that falls on soil affect the amount of soil erosion?

## State a hypothesis.

**1.** Write a **hypothesis** by circling one choice and finishing the sentence.

If more water falls on soil, then *(a) more, (b) less, (c) about the same amount of* soil will be eroded because

.............................................................................

.............................................................................

## Identify and control variables.

**2.** In an **experiment** the variable that you observe is called the **dependent variable** because it changes depending on the variable you change. In this experiment what is the dependent variable?

.............................................................................

**3.** The variable you change is called the **independent variable** because you choose how to change it. It does NOT depend on anything except your choice. What is the independent variable?

.............................................................................

**4.** In an experiment there are factors that could be changed but must not be changed. These are called **controlled variables** because you control the experiment to make sure they do not change. List two controlled variables.

.............................................................................

**4.2.2** Demonstrate and describe how wind, water and glacial ice shape and reshape earth's land surface by eroding rock and soil in some areas and depositing them in other areas in a process that occurs over a long period of time. **4.NS.2** Design a fair test. **4.NS.9** Compare the results of an investigation with the prediction. (Also **4.DP.9**)

## Design your test.

**5.** Draw how you will set up your test.

**6.** List your steps in the order you will do them.

## Do your test.

 **Be careful!** Wear safety goggles.

☑ **7.** Follow the steps you wrote.

☑ **8.** Make sure to **measure** accurately. **Record** your results in a table.

☑ **9.** Scientists repeat their tests to improve their accuracy. Repeat your test if time allows.

**Work Like a Scientist**

Scientists work with other scientists. They compare their methods and results. Talk with your classmates. Compare your methods and results.

## Collect and record your data.

☑ **10.** Fill in the chart.

|  |  |  |
|---|---|---|
|  |  |  |
|  |  |  |
|  |  |  |

# Interpret your data.

☑ **11.** Use your data to make circle graphs.

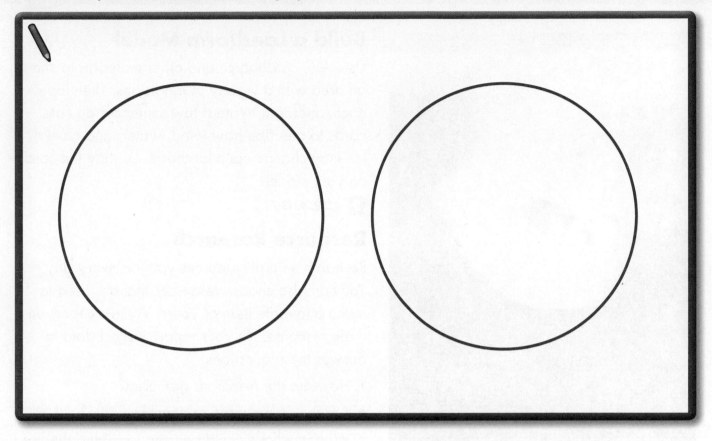

☑ **12.** Look at your graphs closely. Analyze how the amount of water that fell affected the amount of soil the water moved. Identify the evidence you used.

.................................................................................

.................................................................................

.................................................................................

# State your conclusion.

**13. Communicate** your conclusion. Compare your **hypothesis** with your results. Compare your results with others.

.................................................................................

.................................................................................

.................................................................................

## Build a Landform Model

Use clay, cardboard, and other materials to show an area with a variety of landforms. Then label each landform. Write a few sentences on note cards to describe how wind, water, and glacial ice may change each landform. Display the cards on your model.

🌐 4.2.2, 4.NS.7

## Resource Research

Research natural resources you use every day. You can also choose resources that are used to make a favorite item of yours. Write a report on these resources. In your report, collect data to answer these questions:

- How are the resources gathered?
- Are they renewable or nonrenewable?
- What methods could be used to extend the use of these resources?

🌐 4.2.4, 4.2.5

## Write Historical Fiction

Write a historical fiction story about an earthquake, volcano, or landslide that took place in the United States. Write about the time and place of the event. Describe what happened to the surrounding areas during and after the event. Remember that historical fiction uses fictional characters, but tells a story about events that actually happened. Make a model to demonstrate what happened during the event. Your story should include these elements:

- The events before, during, and after the event.
- How the event affected your characters.
- A beginning, middle, and end.

🌐 4.2.3, 4.NS.3, 4.NS.7

### Using Scientific Methods

1. Ask a question.
2. State your hypothesis.
3. Identify and control variables.
4. Test your hypothesis.
5. Collect and record your data.
6. Interpret your data.
7. State your conclusion.
8. Try it again.

# Life Science

## Chapter 6
## Interactions

What do living organisms need to survive?

# Where is this coconut going?

# Interactions

**Try It!**   How can you estimate how many animals live in an ecosystem?

**Investigate It!**   How do earthworms meet their needs in a model of an ecosystem?

You might not recognize it from the grocery store, but this floating seed is a coconut! Coconut seeds are hollow in the center and have thick shells, called husks. Coconuts can float across the water until they wash up on a shore. Then the seed can grow into a new coconut tree.

**Predict**   How do a coconut's hollow center and thick husk help it travel?

......................................................................

......................................................................

**THE BIG Q**   What do living organisms need to survive?

## Inquiry Try It!

### How can you estimate how many animals live in an ecosystem?

Scientists can figure out how many animals live in a large area by counting how many animals there are in small parts of the area and then **estimating.** The more small parts that they check, the better their estimate usually is.

☑ **1.** Scatter two handfuls of cereal on a checkerboard. Guess how many pieces are on the board.

..........................................................................................

☑ **2.** Work with a partner. Determine a way to **estimate** the total number of pieces on the board.

Write your estimate. ...............................................
**Hint:** Start with a small area.

☑ **3.** Count all the pieces of cereal on the board. .....................

### Explain Your Results

**4.** Which was easiest: guessing, **estimating,** or counting?

..........................................................................................

Which was most accurate? .....................................

**5. Infer** How do you think you could make your estimate more accurate?

..........................................................................................

**6.** **Infer** Why do you think scientists might want to know how many animals live in an ecosystem?

..........................................................................................

..........................................................................................

..........................................................................................

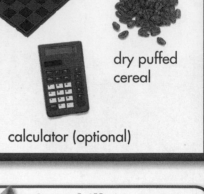

**Materials**

checkerboard

dry puffed cereal

calculator (optional)

**Inquiry Skill** Sometimes you can use math to help you make a good **estimate.**

*checkerboard = ecosystem*

*piece of cereal = animal*

**222**   **4.NS.8** Identify simple patterns in data and propose explanations to account for the patterns.

## Text Features

Text features, such as headings, pictures, and captions, give you clues about what you will read.

Headings tell what the content that follows is about.

A picture shows something you will read about.

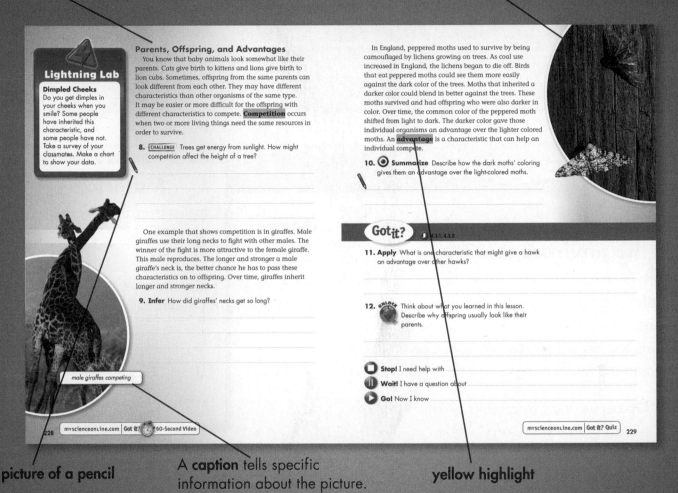

**Lightning Lab**

**Dimpled Cheeks**
Do you get dimples in your cheeks when you smile? Some people have inherited this characteristic, and some people have not. Take a survey of your classmates. Make a chart to show your data.

**Parents, Offspring, and Advantages**
You know that baby animals look somewhat like their parents. Cats give birth to kittens and lions give birth to lion cubs. Sometimes, offspring from the same parents can look different from each other. They may have different characteristics than other organisms of the same type. It may be easier or more difficult for the offspring with different characteristics to compete. **Competition** occurs when two or more living things need the same resources in order to survive.

8. CHALLENGE Trees get energy from sunlight. How might competition affect the height of a tree?

One example that shows competition is in giraffes. Male giraffes use their long necks to fight with other males. The winner of the fight is more attractive to the female giraffe. This male reproduces. The longer and stronger a male giraffe's neck is, the better chance he has to pass these characteristics on to offspring. Over time, giraffes inherit longer and stronger necks.

9. **Infer** How did giraffes' necks get so long?

*male giraffes competing*

228 mYscienceonline.com | Got it? | 60-Second Video

In England, peppered moths used to survive by being camouflaged by lichens growing on trees. As coal use increased in England, the lichens began to die off. Birds that eat peppered moths could see them more easily against the dark color of the trees. Moths that inherited a darker color could blend in better against the trees. These moths survived and had offspring who were also darker in color. Over time, the common color of the peppered moth shifted from light to dark. The darker color gave those individual organisms an advantage over the lighter colored moths. An **advantage** is a characteristic that can help an individual compete.

10. **Summarize** Describe how the dark moths' coloring gives them an advantage over the light-colored moths.

**Got it?** 4.3.1, 4.3.2

11. **Apply** What is one characteristic that might give a hawk an advantage over other hawks?

12. UNLOCK Think about what you learned in this lesson. Describe why offspring usually look like their parents.

⬛ **Stop!** I need help with

⏸ **Wait!** I have a question about

▶ **Go!** Now I know

mYscienceonline.com | Got it? Quiz | 229

picture of a pencil

A **caption** tells specific information about the picture.

yellow highlight

## Practice It!

Find the text features in the textbook pages shown above. Write a clue that each one gives you about the content.

| Text feature | Clue |
|---|---|
|  |  |
|  |  |
|  |  |

## Lesson 1

# What plant and animal characteristics are inherited?

**4.3.1** Observe and describe how offspring are very much, but not exactly, like their parents or one another. Describe how these differences in physical characteristics among individuals in a population may be advantageous for survival and reproduction. (Also **4.3.2 4.NS.8**)

## Envision It!

**Tell** why you think peacocks have inherited showy tails.

**Inquiry** **Explore It!**

## How can some characteristics be affected by the environment?

Many characteristics are inherited. Some are affected by the environment. *A Cards* show living things as they often appear. *B Cards* show how the living things may appear depending on the environment. *C Cards* tell what factors affected the living things.

☑ **1. Observe** the living thing on an *A Card*. Match it with a *B Card*.

☑ **2.** Find the matching *C Card*.

☑ **3.** Repeat for each *A Card*. Compare your matches with others. Explain any differences.

### Materials
Environmental Influence Cards

A Cards          B Cards

C Cards

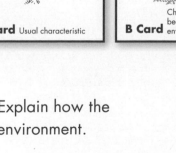

**A Card** Usual characteristic

**B Card** Characteristic that has been affected by an environmental factor

a building

**C Card** Environmental factor

### Explain Your Results

**4. Communicate** Pick an *A Card*. Explain how the characteristic was affected by the environment.

  mysCienceonLine.com | **Explore It! Animation**

 **4.3.4** Describe a way that a given plant or animal might adapt to changes arising from human or non-human impact on the environment. (Also **4.NS.3**)

I will know that plants and animals inherit characteristics that may help them survive and reproduce.

**Words to Know**

characteristics
inherit
competition
advantage

## Characteristics of Living Things

In the middle of the nineteenth century, a monk named Gregor Mendel was hard at work in his garden. He noticed that his pea plants were not all exactly alike. All of the pea plants had stems, leaves, flowers, pods, and peas. But they also had some differences in characteristics. **Characteristics** are the qualities an organism has. Some of the plants were tall while others were short. Some had purple flowers while others had white ones. The pods might be green or yellow. The peas themselves might be smooth or wrinkled.

*pea plant*

The pea plants were like their parents because of characteristics passed on to them. But Mendel found that the offspring did not always look exactly like their parents. Sometimes they received different characteristics. Some offspring even had different characteristics than other plants with the same parents. Mendel asked himself why. Many years later, his work became the basis for the scientific study of heredity, or the passing of characteristics from parents to offspring.

1. **Underline** the different characteristics Mendel's pea plants showed.

2. **Infer** What characteristics will all pea plants have?

........................................................................

........................................................................

## Inherited Characteristics

Animals and plants inherit their characteristics from their parents and look very much like them. In science, to **inherit** is to receive characteristics from an organism's parents. Animals and plants will pass these traits on to their own offspring.

### Plants

The prickly pear cactus has sharp spines. Look at its paddle-shaped pads. These are flattened stems that act like leaves. They have a waxy coating to help the plant hold in moisture. Notice that the pads have two kinds of sharp spines. Some spines are long. Other spines are short but break off easily. The cactus looks the way it does because it has inherited these traits.

3. **Conclude** What characteristic helps the prickly pear cactus survive in a dry environment?

.................................................................................................

.................................................................................................

.................................................................................................

### Animals

You are not likely to mistake a zebra for any other animal. They look like horses, but they are not horses. Zebras have black and white stripes. Their manes are short and stand up on their necks. These are inherited characteristics. They are shared by all zebras.

4. **Analyze** How is a zebra's pattern like a fingerprint?

.................................................................................................

.................................................................................................

.................................................................................................

*The general coat pattern is shared by zebras of the same kind. The pattern of each individual zebra is different.*

5. **◉ Text Features** Find five text features on these pages. Tell a partner the clues they give you.

Did you look twice at the fish in the photo? Something does not look quite right. The peacock flounder has both eyes on one side of its body! This flat fish is unusual in another way too. The peacock flounder can change its color and pattern to match its background. This allows it to surprise the animals it eats as they swim by. It also hides itself from animals that would eat it. This fish looks and acts the way it does because it has inherited these traits.

6. ◉ **Summarize** List three characteristics that the peacock flounder inherited.

........................................................................

........................................................................

........................................................................

## Human Beings

People also inherit many characteristics from their parents. A person's parents may be very tall, and so that person may grow to be very tall also. However, this is not always the case. Sometimes a child may grow up to be taller or shorter than his or her parents. Height is not the only inherited characteristic. Some characteristics such as hair and eye color are also inherited.

7. **Give an Example** Write a characteristic you may have inherited from your parents.

........................................................................

........................................................................

# Lightning Lab

## Dimpled Cheeks
Do you get dimples in your cheeks when you smile? Some people have inherited this characteristic, and some people have not. Take a survey of your classmates. Make a chart to show your data.

## Parents, Offspring, and Advantages

You know that baby animals look somewhat like their parents. Cats give birth to kittens and lions give birth to lion cubs. Sometimes, offspring from the same parents can look different from each other. They may have different characteristics than other organisms of the same type. It may be easier or more difficult for the offspring with different characteristics to compete. **Competition** occurs when two or more living things need the same resources in order to survive.

8. [CHALLENGE] Trees get energy from sunlight. How might competition affect the height of a tree?

........................................................................

........................................................................

........................................................................

........................................................................

One example that shows competition is in giraffes. Male giraffes use their long necks to fight with other males. The winner of the fight is more attractive to the female giraffe. This male reproduces. The longer and stronger a male giraffe's neck is, the better chance he has to pass these characteristics on to offspring. Over time, giraffes inherit longer and stronger necks.

9. **Infer** How did giraffes' necks get so long?

........................................................................

........................................................................

........................................................................

........................................................................

male giraffes competing

myscienceonline.com | Got it? | 60-Second Video

In England, peppered moths used to survive by being camouflaged by lichens growing on trees. As coal use increased in England, the lichens began to die off. Birds that eat peppered moths could see them more easily against the dark color of the trees. Moths that inherited a darker color could blend in better against the trees. These moths survived and had offspring who were also darker in color. Over time, the common color of the peppered moth shifted from light to dark. The darker color gave those individual organisms an advantage over the lighter colored moths. An **advantage** is a characteristic that can help an individual compete.

10. ● **Summarize** Describe how the dark moths' coloring gives them an advantage over the light-colored moths.

....................................................................................

....................................................................................

**Got it?**   ① 4.3.1, 4.3.2

11. **Apply** What is one characteristic that might give a hawk an advantage over other hawks?

....................................................................................

....................................................................................

12. **UNLOCK THE BIG Q** Think about what you learned in this lesson. Describe why offspring usually look like their parents.

....................................................................................

....................................................................................

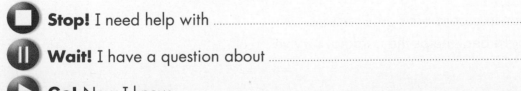

⬛ **Stop!** I need help with ..................................................................

⏸ **Wait!** I have a question about ....................................................

▶ **Go!** Now I know ....................................................................

# What are adaptations?

bald eagle

4.3.2 Observe, compare, and record the physical characteristics of living plants or animals from widely different environments, and describe how each is adapted to its environment. (Also 4.NS.7)

**Tell** how you think the feet of each bird shown above help it survive in its habitat.

## Inquiry Explore It!

### Which bird beak can crush seeds?

☑ 1. **Make a model** of a heron's beak. Glue 2 craft sticks to a clothespin. Use the other clothespin as a model of a cardinal's beak. Use pieces of a straw as models of seeds.

☑ 2. Use the heron's beak. Pick up a seed. Does the beak crush the seed? Try 5 times. **Record.**

_____  _____  _____  _____

☑ 3. Repeat with the cardinal's beak. Record.

_____  _____  _____  _____

### Explain Your Results

4. **Draw a Conclusion**
   Which bird crushes seeds?

...............................................................................

5. There are many seeds in a cardinal's environment. **Infer** how a cardinal's beak helps the cardinal survive.

...............................................................................

...............................................................................

**Materials**

4 pieces of straw

2 clothespins

craft sticks

glue

myscienceonline.com | Explore It! Animation

4.NS.3 Plan and carry out investigations as a class, in small groups or independently, often over a period of several class lessons.

mallard duck

I will know how physical features and behaviors help organisms interact with their environments.

## Words to Know

adaptation     environment

## Adaptations

Animals and plants inherit characteristics from their parents. These special features and behaviors help them survive. An **adaptation** is a physical feature or behavior that helps an organism survive in its environment. An **environment** is everything that surrounds a living thing. Organisms with useful adaptations for their environment are more likely than other organisms to get the resources they need to survive. If they survive, they are more likely to reproduce and pass their adaptations to their young.

Plants and animals in different ecosystems often have different adaptations. A plant or animal adapted to one ecosystem may not survive in a different ecosystem. Hares that live in snowy environments have different adaptations from hares that live in a desert. So, a hare from a snowy environment might not survive in a desert.

1. ◉ **Text Features** Complete the chart below to identify some text features on this page.

| Feature | Clue |
|---------|------|
| heading | The heading tells that the paragraphs are about adaptations. |
| picture | |

snowshoe hare

2. **Explain** How do you think the snowshoe hare in the picture is adapted to live in an environment that has a lot of snow?

..........................................
..........................................
..........................................
..........................................
..........................................

## Adaptations in Ecosystems

There are several different ecosystems in North America, such as tundra, rain forest, desert, grassland, and forest. Some ecosystems are cold and dry, while others are warm and wet. Some ecosystems have sandy soil, while others have fertile soil. The plants and animals that live in an area are adapted to the climate and soil. Organisms can survive only in environments in which their needs are met. In any environment, some kinds of plants and animals survive better than others.

For example, you may think that nothing can live in a desert ecosystem, but deserts have many organisms living there. Cacti and some lizards are adapted to live in deserts. The desert horned lizard uses sandy soil as a hiding place. The lizard can quickly become invisible by throwing sand over its body.

3. **Interpret** Read the descriptions of different ecosystems to the right. Write three adaptations organisms have to live in these ecosystems.

.........................................................

.........................................................

.........................................................

.........................................................

4. [CHALLENGE] How might grassland organisms respond if very little precipitation falls on the grassland for several years?

.........................................................

.........................................................

.........................................................

.........................................................

## Wetlands ⑤

In wetlands, the ground is covered with water for at least part of the year. Water lilies and cypress trees grow in some wetlands. Raccoons in wetlands survive by eating insects, fish, amphibians, and some kinds of plants.

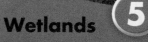

*raccoon*

mysCienceonLine.com | I Will Know...

## ① Tundra

A tundra is a cold region. The ground beneath the surface is frozen all year. Some grasses can grow, but trees cannot. Caribou have two layers of fur to help keep them warm.

*caribou*

## ② Rain Forest

Not all rain forests are tropical. The mild and rainy climate of the Pacific Northwest supports temperate rain forests. The northern spotted owl survives in the mild climate. It is able to catch prey all year.

*northern spotted owl*

## ③ Desert

The driest ecosystem is a desert. Some plants and animals have adapted to the limited water supply. The desert horned lizard's coloring helps it blend in to avoid predators and to catch prey.

## ④ Grassland

Grasslands, as their name suggests, are covered with grasses. They receive a medium amount of rain. Grasshoppers are often difficult to see in grasslands, which helps them hide from predators.

*grasshopper*

*desert horned lizard*

## Animal Adaptations

Animals have many adaptations that help them survive in their environments. Some adaptations, such as sharp beaks, teeth, or claws, may help them get food. Other adaptations, such as stingers, quills, smelly sprays, or bitter-tasting flesh, protect some animals from being eaten by predators. Bright colors, like those of the monarch butterfly, may warn predators that the animal is poisonous.

Some adaptations for moving help an animal protect itself. For example, fins enable a fish to swim away from its enemies. Birds' wings help them quickly move if they need to get away from predators or cold weather.

Hibernation, or a state of rest, is a behavior that helps some animals survive low temperatures. Some animals that hibernate include bears, chipmunks, and marmots.

**5. Describe** Write a caption about an adaptation this tiger has. Include how you think the adaptation helps the tiger survive.

.................................................................................................................

.................................................................................................................

6. **Classify** Read about the animals on this page. (Circle) the names of the animals with adaptations for getting food. **Underline** the names of the animals with adaptations for protection.

The porcupine lives in grasslands and other areas. Its quills are very sharp. The quills protect the porcupine against predators.

This poison-dart frog lives in a South American rain forest. Its bright color warns predators that it is poisonous.

This flying gecko lives in the jungle forest. It has flaps of skin that help it to glide away from predators.

This red-tailed hawk hunts in forests and fields. It has a sharp, curved beak that can hold and tear prey it finds.

Chameleons live in deserts and tropical areas. Their long tongues stretch to catch insects.

7. **Observe and Compare** Look at the animals on these pages. Describe to a partner how each is adapted to its environment. Tell how their physical characteristics are alike.

## Plant Adaptations

Like animals, plants have many adaptations that help them survive in their environments. Some adaptations, such as cactus thorns, protect plants from harm. Other adaptations help plants reproduce. These adaptations may help plants pollinate or spread their seeds.

Adaptations such as harmful oils and thorns may protect a plant from being eaten. Other adaptations allow plants to survive in extreme conditions. For example, sundew plants that live in nutrient-poor soil have a sticky substance that attracts insects. These insects provide nutrients to the plant.

8. **Apply** The hairs on a stinging nettle release a chemical that irritates skin. Write a caption that explains how this adaptation helps the plant.

.......................................................................................

.......................................................................................

This burdock bush has seeds with spikes that stick to furry animals that brush against them.

Cactus plants live in deserts where there is little rain. They have tiny needle-like leaves and a thick waxy coating on their stem that keeps them from drying out.

Some flowering plants depend on insects or other animals to pollinate their flowers. This is how they make new plants. The flower of a bee orchid looks like a bee. This adaptation helps the orchid attract insects.

bee orchid

9. **Illustrate** Draw another plant you know. Describe an adaptation the plant has and how it helps the plant.

...........................................................................................................

...........................................................................................................

**Got it?**

🕐 4.3.2, 4.NS.7

10. **Describe** How is a cactus adapted to its habitat?

...........................................................................................................

...........................................................................................................

...........................................................................................................

11. **Analyze** How is a duck adapted to help it survive in its environment?

...........................................................................................................

...........................................................................................................

⏹ **Stop!** I need help with .........................................................

⏸ **Wait!** I have a question about ..........................................

▶ **Go!** Now I know .................................................................

# Lesson 3

## How do living things respond to environments?

**Envision It!**

⓿ 4.3.3 Design an investigation to explore how organisms meet some of their needs by responding to stimuli from their environment.

**Write** one way you think this plant might hurt the meadow environment.

# my planeT DiaRY

## /// MISCONCEPTION ///

Have you ever heard that bats cannot see? A common misconception about bats is that they are blind. Some bats use something called echolocation to locate prey, such as insects. Echolocation uses sound energy. Bats make a sound and then hear the echo as it bounces off an object, such as a delicious mosquito. Then the bat knows how far away and in what direction the insect is flying. Because bats can find prey in the dark, many people have assumed they were blind. But all types of bats have eyes that can see. They can only see in black, white, and shades of gray.

How can bats get information from their environments?

...................................................................

...................................................................

...................................................................

...................................................................

...................................................................

**Word to Know**

stimulus

## Environmental Characteristics

All organisms live in environments. The weather conditions in an area, food supply, and types of shelter are all parts of an organism's environment. Organisms use the resources in their environments to grow and survive.

The characteristics of an environment affect the organisms that live there. Some environments have characteristics that are different in different seasons. An organism that lives in this type of environment may change its structure or behavior throughout the year. For example, some trees shed their leaves in the winter. This may help the trees to conserve water and survive cold conditions. Some animals, such as the cedar waxwing, move out of an environment when the season changes. Some cedar waxwings spend their summers in Canada. They fly south for the winter and return north in the spring. In this way, the cedar waxwing can best meet its needs.

1. ◎ **Text Features**
What is the passage about? What text feature helped you find out?

.................................................
.................................................
.................................................
.................................................

cedar waxwing

mysceienceonLine.com | **Envision It!**

239

## Response to Conditions in Environments

Plants and animals need to meet their needs to be able to survive. Sometimes organisms change depending on the conditions in their environment. These changes may help the organisms meet their needs. These changes may also be a result of the organisms meeting their needs.

### Animals

Close your eyes. Think of a flamingo. What color is it? You probably thought of a pink flamingo. Flamingos actually have white feathers. The pink or red color comes from their diet. Flamingos eat foods such as shrimp and algae. These foods are rich in a substance called carotene. Carotene turns the flamingos' white feathers pink or red.

2. **Explain** How does a flamingo's diet change its characteristics?

........................................................................

........................................................................

Sometimes an environment can affect an animal even before it is born or hatched. In some reptiles, including sea turtles, the temperature of the eggs in a nest makes a difference. If the nest is warm, many more females will develop. If the nest is cooler, many more males will develop. Even temperature differences within the same nest can make a difference.

3. **Predict** If eggs at the top of a sea-turtle nest are warm and eggs at the bottom of the nest are cooler, what might happen to the eggs in the middle of the nest?

........................................................................

........................................................................

........................................................................

myscienceonline.com | THE BIG | I Will Know...

## Plants

Plants are also affected by their environment. For example, some trees grow best in a certain type of soil. Trees growing in windy areas may grow sideways if the wind always blows in the same direction. The wind is a stimulus. A **stimulus** (plural: stimuli) is something that causes a reaction in a living thing.

A potted plant is also an environment. Bonsai is a method for growing miniature trees. Gardeners control the amount of nutrients and water the trees receive. The gardeners change bonsai trees' environments, which change the trees' characteristics. If a bonsai tree grew to a normal size, it would not be able to meet its needs in a small pot.

4. **Summarize** How does a gardener shape a bonsai tree's environment?

.......................................................................................

.......................................................................................

## Do the math!

### Estimating Height

Suppose the height of a Japanese red-maple bonsai tree is 28 cm. A full-size Japanese red-maple tree is 31 times as tall. About how tall is the full-size tree?

Use **rounding** to estimate the height.

**28** cm × **31**

Round 28 to 30.
Round 31 to 30.

**30** cm × **30** = **900** cm

The full-size tree is about 900 cm tall.

1. A bonsai fir tree is 18 cm tall. A full-size fir tree is 97 times as tall. Estimate the height of the full-size fir tree and explain your answer. Show your work.

Japanese red-maple bonsai tree

## Meeting Needs in Environments

How an organism interacts with its environment can affect how its needs are met. Organisms may change their behavior depending on the conditions in an environment.

### Animals Meeting Needs

An important need of living things is shelter. Animals such as the house sparrow have learned some useful ways to find good places to build nests. Some house sparrows learned how to trigger the sensor that opens automatic doors! You may have seen these doors when you go to stores. The birds open the doors and then fly in and make nests inside. In this way, the sparrows avoid predators and harsh weather conditions.

You may know that your body temperature stays at about 37°C when you are healthy. This is true whether you are in a warm or cold room. Some animals rely on their environment to regulate their body temperature. One example is the sea star. During low tide, the water gets shallower near the coastline. There is less water for sunlight to go through, so the ocean floor can heat up more during low tide. The sea star prepares for this time of extra warmth by sucking in cold water during high tide. Then the cooler water inside the animal keeps its temperature from rising too high when the tide lowers.

house sparrow

5. **Calculate** A Caribbean sea star survives best when its body temperature is 24°C. How much cooler is its body temperature than yours? Show your work.

sea star

myscienceonline.com | Got it? | 60-Second Video

## Plants Meeting Needs

Plants need energy from sunlight to produce food. To meet this need, some plants have the ability to change their direction of growth. You may have seen a plant bend towards a source of light. Light is a stimulus for these plants. Some plants, such as climbing ivies, grow up tree trunks or walls. The ivy senses the object, and it changes its growth to climb. In this way, ivy better meets its need for light and space. Touch is a stimulus for these plants.

climbing ivy

6. ◎ **Sequence** Draw to complete the sequence below.

Let the plant grow.

Turn the pot around.

Predict.

# Got it?

○ 4.3.3

7. **Give an Example** Write two ways living things might change to meet their needs in an environment.

......................................................................................................

......................................................................................................

8. **UNLOCK THE BIG Q** Female mallard ducks often build their nests on the ground. Their feathers are the same color as the ground. List two ways they are interacting with their environment.

......................................................................................................

......................................................................................................

⬛ **Stop!** I need help with ..........................................................

❚❚ **Wait!** I have a question about ..............................................

▶ **Go!** Now I know ....................................................................

## Lesson 4

# How do living things respond to change?

4.3.4 Describe a way that a given plant or animal might adapt to changes arising from human or non-human impact on the environment.

### Envision It!

**Tell** how humans have affected this deer's environment.

---

## Inquiry Explore It!

### How can pollution affect an organism?

☑ **1. Measure**  Add 30 mL of water to Cup A.
Add 30 mL of vinegar to Cup B.

☑ **2.** Add 1 spoonful of sugar and $\frac{1}{2}$ spoonful of yeast to both cups. Stir gently.

30 mL water
$\frac{1}{2}$ spoonful yeast
1 spoonful sugar

30 mL vinegar
$\frac{1}{2}$ spoonful yeast
1 spoonful sugar

☑ **3.** Put the cups in a warm place.

☑ **4. Observe** the yeast after 5, 10, and 15 minutes.

### Explain Your Results

**5. Infer**  Which cup is a **model** of a polluted habitat for yeast? Explain.

.................................................

.................................................

## Materials

safety goggles

2 plastic cups

graduated cylinder

vinegar

water

spoon

yeast

sugar

clock

mysCienceonLine.com | Explore It! Animation

4.NS.8 Identify simple patterns in data and propose explanations to account for the patterns. (Also 4.3.3, 4.3.4)

I will recognize that plants, animals, and humans can affect the environment.

**Word to Know**

nonnative

## Changes to the Environment

The environment is like a balance. One side holds what lives in the environment. The other side holds resources that the environment provides. If the environment provides enough resources to support life, the balance is level.

Change often tips the balance. For example, tree seeds may sprout on a log and start to grow. The young trees need light and space to grow. The young trees are in competition. Competition occurs when two or more living things need the same resources in order to survive. Some trees get enough light. As their branches grow, they shade nearby plants. The environment changes. Other young trees may not get enough light to survive.

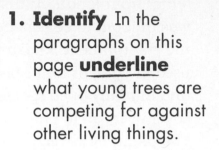

1. **Identify** In the paragraphs on this page **underline** what young trees are competing for against other living things.

2. **Examine** How can the fallen tree in this picture change a forest habitat?

........................................

........................................

........................................

........................................

........................................

........................................

........................................

........................................

## Plants Cause Change

Changes can help some living things and harm others. For example, a plant called purple loosestrife was brought to the United States. No animals eat this plant. It is spreading to new places. That's great for the loosestrife! However, there is less space for other plants to grow. Some kinds of plants are completely pushed out of the environment.

A plant called kudzu was originally brought to the United States from Japan. At first, kudzu was thought to be beneficial to the environment. Kudzu was used in gardens for its beauty and in many open spaces as a cover over soil to prevent erosion. The plant, however, grows very well in the southeastern United States. Because the vines grow so well, they destroy forests by blocking trees' sunlight. Both purple loosestrife and kudzu are nonnative plants. **Nonnative** organisms live outside of their usual habitats. When this happens, it can result in no natural predators that keep the species in balance.

*purple loosestrife*

*kudzu*

3. **Summarize** How has kudzu both helped and harmed habitats?

.................................................................

.................................................................

.................................................................

.................................................................

.................................................................

.................................................................

246

## Animals Cause Change

Some animals change the environment to improve their habitat. Beavers, for example, need deep water. If the stream where they live is too shallow, the beavers build a pond. They cut down trees with their teeth. They use the wood to build a dam across the stream. The blocked water forms a pond behind the dam.

The change helps plants and animals that need to live in still water. Also, the trees the beavers cut down no longer shade the ground below. Small plants and shrubs that benefit from direct sunlight grow in their place.

The change harms plants and animals whose homes are flooded. Trees needed to make the dam are lost. The pond also takes homes away from plants and animals that prefer the flowing water of streams.

**4. Conclude** This habitat was once a grassy meadow. How has this beaver dam changed it?

.................................................................................

.................................................................................

.................................................................................

.................................................................................

A beaver can cut down over 200 trees per year!

A beaver can add over 5 feet of length to its dam per day.

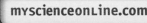

**5. Visualize** This bridge was built in and over an aquatic ecosystem. Describe how you think this bridge affected the plants and animals living in the area.

...................................................................

...................................................................

...................................................................

...................................................................

...................................................................

...................................................................

## Humans Cause Change

People need resources just as other living things do. When people build homes, they change the environment. They might cut down trees in forests or plow up grasslands to make room for houses. Each of these changes affects the environment.

Sometimes animals and humans compete for space. People move to places where animals live. Then they might find coyotes in their backyards or a deer strolling onto the lanes of a busy highway. Other people build birdhouses and put them in their backyards. This provides shelter for birds in the area.

6. **Explain** What are some ways that the people who built this birdhouse affected the environment?

..................................................................................

..................................................................................

..................................................................................

Got it?   **(i)** 4.3.4

7. **Compare** How do beavers and people impact their environments?

..................................................................................

..................................................................................

8. **UNLOCK THE BIG Q** Think about what you learned in this lesson. Are changes to the environment always harmful?

..................................................................................

..................................................................................

..................................................................................

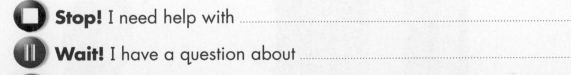

■ **Stop!** I need help with .............................................................

❙❙ **Wait!** I have a question about ................................................

▶ **Go!** Now I know .......................................................................

## How do earthworms meet their needs in a model of an ecosystem?

### Follow a Procedure

☑ **1.** Obtain an earthworm bottle from your teacher. Use a spoon to add a thin layer of sand. Add 6 worms.

**Be careful!** Earthworms are living organisms. Handle with care.

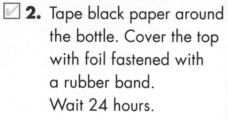

☑ **2.** Tape black paper around the bottle. Cover the top with foil fastened with a rubber band. Wait 24 hours.

### Materials

earthworm bottle

spoon

foil

plastic cup with sand

black paper

rubber band

6 earthworms

masking tape

### Inquiry Skill

Scientists make careful observations and record data accurately. They use their data to help make **inferences.**

**4.3.2** Observe, compare, and record the physical characteristics of living plants or animals from widely different environments, and describe how each is adapted to its environment. (Also **4.3.3**, **4.NS.3**)

**3.** Remove the paper and foil. **Observe** the sand, dirt, and earthworms. **Record** your observations.

### Earthworm Observations

| Day | Observations |
|---|---|
| **Day 1** (24 hours after making ecosystem) | |
| **Day 2** | |
| **Day 3** |  |
| **Day 4** | |

**4.** Replace the paper and the foil. Observe daily for 3 more days. Record your observations.

Be careful! Wash your hands when finished.

## Analyze and Conclude

**5.** Explain your **observations.**

............................................................................................................

............................................................................................................

**6. Infer** Do the earthworms get what they need from the ecosystem? Tell how you know.

............................................................................................................

............................................................................................................

**7.**  What does the model ecosystem show about how living things interact in their environment?

............................................................................................................

............................................................................................................

🔵 4.3.2

# Wildlife Biologist

If you like animals, you might like to be a wildlife biologist. Wildlife biologists study animals and their habitats. They want to know how the animals live and how they behave.

At the International Crane Foundation (ICF) near Baraboo, Wisconsin, biologists study cranes in captivity and in the wild. With the information the biologists gather, they hope to increase the number of these endangered birds.

One important job the biologists have is to reteach cranes to migrate. The urge to migrate is an instinctive behavior. However, the migration route must be learned. Cranes raised in captivity do not know where to go. Biologists fly small aircraft and train the cranes to follow them.

If you think wildlife biology is for you, plan to take science classes in high school. You might volunteer to work with animals in a local habitat. You will need a college degree in biology or a related science.

APPLY THE BIG Q

How does a captive environment affect the cranes' migration characteristic?

# Vocabulary Smart Cards

characteristics
inherit
competition
advantage
adaptation
environment
stimulus
nonnative

## Play a Game!

Cut out the Vocabulary Smart Cards.

Work with a partner. Choose a Vocabulary Smart Card. Say as many words as you can think of that describe that vocabulary word.

Have your partner guess the word.

**advantage**

ventaja

**characteristics**

rasgos

**adaptation**

fur turns white in the winter

adaptación

**inherit**

heredar

**environment**

snowy forest

medio ambiente

**competition**

competencia

the qualities an organism has

Write an example.

..............................

..............................

..............................

cualidades que tiene un organismo

---

a characteristic that can help an individual compete

Write a synonym for this word

..............................

..............................

..............................

característica que le permite a un individuo competir

---

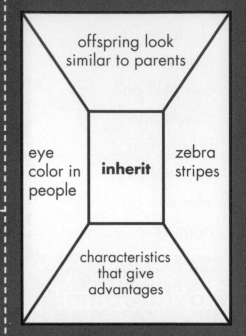

offspring look similar to parents

eye color in people | **inherit** | zebra stripes

characteristics that give advantages

## Make a Word Frame

Choose a vocabulary word and write it in the center of the frame. Write or draw details about the vocabulary word in the spaces around it.

---

to receive characteristics from an organism's parents

Write an example.

..............................

..............................

..............................

recibir rasgos de los padres de un organismo

---

a physical feature or behavior that helps an organism survive in its environment

Write an example.

..............................

..............................

rasgo físico o forma de conducta que ayuda a un organismo a sobrevivir en su medio ambiente

---

occurs when two or more living things need the same resources in order to survive

Write a sentence using the verb form of this word.

..............................

..............................

ocurre cuando dos o más seres vivos necesitan los mismos recursos para sobrevivir

---

everything that surrounds a living thing

What is an everyday meaning of this word?

..............................

..............................

..............................

todo lo que rodea a un ser vivo

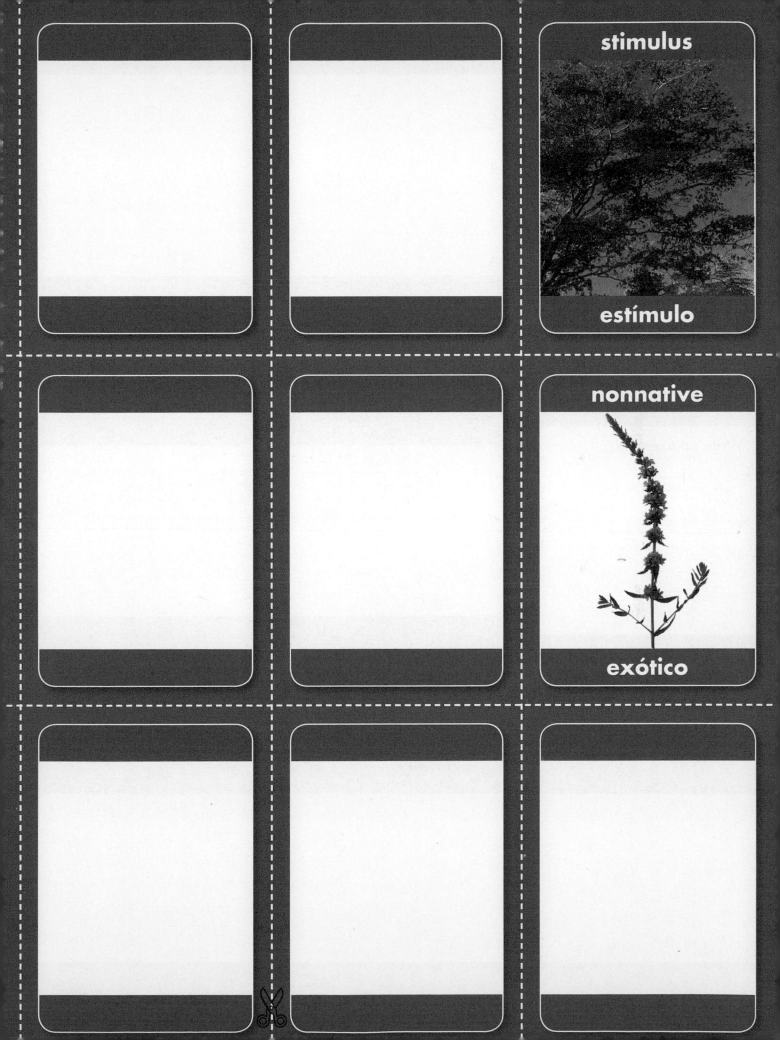

**stimulus**

**estímulo**

**nonnative**

**exótico**

something that causes a
reaction in a living thing

Write an example.

.............................

.............................

.............................

.............................

algo que provoca una
reacción en un ser vivo

---

organisms that live outside
of their usual habitats

Write an example.

.............................

.............................

.............................

.............................

organismo que vive fuera
de su hábitat natural

**Lesson 1**

### What plant and animal characteristics are inherited?

- Organisms inherit some characteristics from their parents.
- Some characteristics give an individual an advantage over other individuals.

**Lesson 2**

### What are adaptations?

- Adaptations help organisms survive in their environments.
- Some adaptations help animals get food or protect themselves.
- Some adaptations help plants survive or reproduce.

**Lesson 3**

### How do living things respond to environments?

- An environment is everything that surrounds a living thing.
- Organisms interact with their environments to meet their needs.
- Some organisms change their behavior to survive in environments.

**Lesson 4**

### How do living things respond to change?

- Living things compete with each other for food and space.
- Some animals change their environment to better meet their needs.
- Changes in the environment help some living things and harm others.

What do living organisms need to survive?

---

## Lesson 1  4.3.1, 4.3.2, 4.NS.8

### What plant and animal characteristics are inherited?

1. **Explain** What does it mean to inherit a characteristic?

_____

_____

_____

2. **Vocabulary** A characteristic of an organism that helps it survive better than other organisms without the characteristic is called a(n):
   A. competition
   B. advantage
   C. characteristic
   D. environment

3. **Give an Example** Write one characteristic that humans inherit from their parents.

_____

_____

4. **Identify** Which of the following is NOT an inherited characteristic?
   A. the shape of a maple leaf
   B. the color of a panda's fur
   C. a polar bear learning to hunt
   D. the height of a pea plant

---

## Lesson 2  4.3.2, 4.NS.7

### What are adaptations?

5. **Write About It** Give an example of a type of environment. Write about two types of adaptations organisms have in that environment.

_____

_____

_____

_____

_____

_____

6. **Vocabulary** In which type of ecosystem does this animal probably live?

   A. tundra (cold, dry)
   B. wetland (warm, humid)
   C. savannah (hot, usually dry)
   D. tropical rainforest (hot, humid)

 **Lesson 3** 🔵 4.3.3

**How do living things respond to environments?**

7. 🔘 **Text Features**

### Response by Organisms

Some plants and animals change their behavior or physical appearance in response to their environment. These changes may or may not help the organism meet its needs. For example, a hydrangea plant will have either blue or pink flowers, depending on the condition of the soil. This does not help or harm the plant.

What is the heading of this reading selection?

.................................................

.................................................

.................................................

8. **Analyze** In what ways can other living things in a plant's environment affect its characteristics?

.................................................

.................................................

.................................................

.................................................

**Lesson 4** 🔵 4.3.4

**How do living things respond to change?**

9. **Suggest** What is one way humans can affect an environment in a positive way?

.................................................

.................................................

.................................................

.................................................

.................................................

.................................................

10.  **What do living organisms need to survive?**

Think about a newly-hatched gosling. A gosling is a young goose. After the gosling has hatched, how does it grow? How does it know what to do?

.................................................

.................................................

.................................................

.................................................

.................................................

# Indiana ISTEP+ Practice

## Multiple Choice

**1** Which of the following changes can have an effect on a plant or animal in its environment?

   A. introduction of nonnative plants

   B. beavers building a dam

   C. humans building a house

   D. all of the above

            **4.3.1**

## Constructed Response

**2** Eastern bluebirds look for prey from high above the ground. Look at the drawing of a typical insect that is prey for the eastern bluebird. Describe one insect adaptation that might have occurred over time.

            **4.3.4**

## Extended Response

**3** Suppose you want to observe how the temperature changes throughout the year affect the appearance of an outdoor plant. What is one hypothesis you might form?

Write a procedure to test your hypothesis.

            **4.NS.1**

# Biography

# Rachel Carson

In the 1950s, people used a chemical called DDT to poison harmful insects. Farmers sprayed it on their fields. In cities and towns, it was used on the plants in parks.

Rachel Carson was a scientist and a writer. She began to notice that every spring there were fewer and fewer songbirds. She wondered what was happening to the bird populations. After making careful observations, Carson learned that DDT was building up on land and in lakes and streams. The chemical had entered the food chains and webs of many ecosystems.

Carson wanted to warn as many people as possible about the dangers of using DDT. In 1962 she wrote a book titled *Silent Spring*. Because of her book, laws forbidding the use of DDT were passed. Society has been more aware of the delicate balance of ecosystems ever since.

APPLY THE BIG Q

How do you think the interaction of DDT in the environment affected the birds?

## Materials

small plastic tub

2 sponges

water

plastic spoon

plastic cup of sand

10 mealworms and food

# Do mealworms prefer damp or dry places?

A mealworm can sense whether the environment is damp or dry. Sometimes conditions change. You will **experiment** to find out how the environment affects mealworms' behavior.

## Ask a question.

Do mealworms prefer to live in a damp place or a dry place?

## State a hypothesis.

**1.** Write a **hypothesis** by circling one choice and finishing the sentence.

If mealworms can move to a damp place or a dry place, then they will move to a place that is

*(a) damp*

*(b) dry*

because

..............................................................................................

..............................................................................................

..............................................................................................

## Identify and control variables.

**2.** In this experiment you will observe where the mealworms move. You must change only one variable. Everything else must remain the same. What should stay the same? List two examples.

..............................................................................................

..............................................................................................

**3.** Tell the one change you will make.

..............................................................................................

..............................................................................................

**4.3.3** Design an investigation to explore how organisms meet some of their needs by responding to stimuli from their environment. **4.NS.2** Design a fair test. **4.NS.8** Identify simple patterns in data and propose explanations to account for the patterns. **4.DP.9** Present evidence using mathematical representations (graphs, data tables). (Also **4.3.4, 4.NS.9**)

## Design your test.

☑ **4.** Draw how you will set up your test.

☑ **5.** List your steps in the order you will do them.

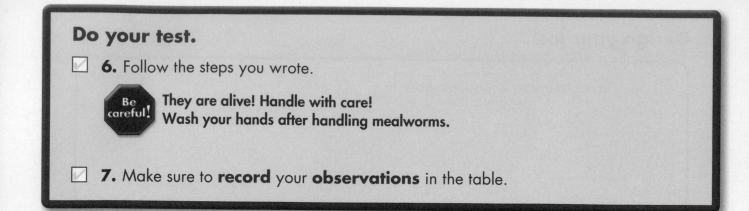

## Do your test.

☑ **6.** Follow the steps you wrote.

**Be careful!** They are alive! Handle with care!
Wash your hands after handling mealworms.

☑ **7.** Make sure to **record** your **observations** in the table.

## Collect and record your data.

☑ **8.** Fill in the chart.

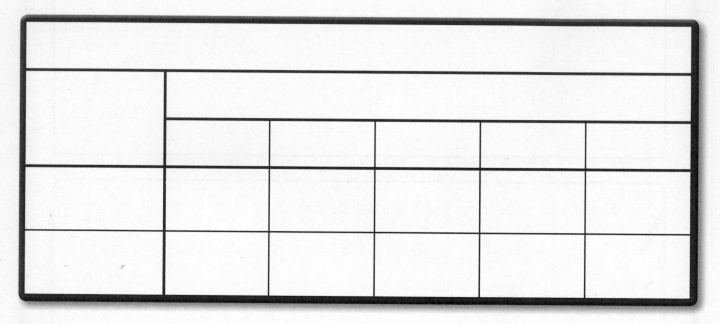

Check to see if your data are reasonable. You started
with 10 mealworms. Each day add up the total number
of mealworms. Make sure the total is 10.

### Work Like a Scientist

Scientists work with other
scientists. Compare your
observations with other groups.
Seek reasons that might explain
any differences.

# Interpret your data.

☑ **9.** Use your data to make bar graphs.

☑ **10.** Compare what you see in the 2 graphs.

..........................................................................

..........................................................................

..........................................................................

..........................................................................

## State your conclusion.

**11. Communicate** your conclusion. Compare your **hypothesis** with your results. Share your results with others.

..........................................................................

..........................................................................

..........................................................................

..........................................................................

**Technology Tools**

Your teacher may want you to use a computer (with the right software) or a graphing calculator to help collect, organize, analyze, and present your data. These tools can help you make tables, charts, and graphs.

## Build a Model of an Ecosystem

Choose one type of ecosystem you have read about. Use a cardboard box, clay, construction paper, foam, or other materials to build a model of your ecosystem. Include labeled models of living and nonliving things. Write about the adaptations of the plants and animals in your ecosystem.

🅓 **4.3.2, 4.NS.3, 4.NS.7**

## Write a Biography

Choose an animal found in your state, and write a biography for the animal. Be sure to include these things:

• The type of animal

• The animal's ecosystem and habitat

• The adaptations that help the animal survive in its environment

• Ways the animal responds to changes in its environment

🅓 **4.3.1**

## Make a Presentation

Like beavers, humans build dams that change the flow of rivers. Research some dams in your state to find out more about how dams change environments. Find or draw pictures of one dam to show in a presentation to your class. Write captions for the pictures, explaining how the dam affects the environment. Share your findings in your presentation.

🅓 **4.3.4, 4.NS.7**

## Using Scientific Methods

1. Ask a question.

2. State your hypothesis.

3. Identify and control variables.

4. Test your hypothesis.

5. Collect and record your data.

6. Interpret your data.

7. State your conclusion.

8. Try it again.

266

# Measurements

## Metric and Customary Measurements

The metric system is the measurement system most commonly used in science. Metric units are sometimes called SI units. SI stands for International System. It is called that because these units are used around the world.

1 liter

These prefixes are used in the metric system:

*kilo-* means *thousand*
1 kilometer = 1,000 meters

*milli-* means *one thousandth*
1,000 millimeters = 1 meter, or 1 millimeter = 0.001 meter

1 cup

*centi-* means *one hundredth*
100 centimeters = 1 meter, or 1 centimeter = 0.01 meter

**Temperature**
Water freezes at 0°C, or 32°F.
Water boils at 100°C, or 212°F.

1 pound

1 kilogram

**Volume**
One liter is greater than 4 cups.

**Mass**
One kilogram is greater than 2 pounds.

1 meter

1 yard

**Length and Distance**
One meter is longer than 1 yard.

# Glossary

The glossary uses letters and signs to show how words are pronounced. The mark ′ is placed after a syllable with a primary or heavy accent. The mark ′ is placed after a syllable with a secondary or lighter accent.

To hear these vocabulary words and definitions, you can refer to the AudioText CD, or log on to the digital path's Vocabulary Smart Cards.

## Pronunciation Key

| | | |
|---|---|---|
| a  in hat | ō  in open | sh  in she |
| ā  in age | ȯ  in all | th  in thin |
| â  in care | ô  in order | ŦH  in then |
| ä  in far | oi  in oil | zh  in measure |
| e  in let | ou  in out | ə = a in about |
| ē  in equal | u  in cup | ə = e in taken |
| ėr  in term | u̇  in put | ə = i in pencil |
| i  in it | ü  in rule | ə = o in lemon |
| ī  in ice | ch  in child | ə = u in circus |
| o  in hot | ng  in long | |

## A

**adaptation** (ad′ ap tā′ shən) a physical feature or behavior that helps an organism survive in its environment

**adaptación** rasgo físico o forma de conducta que ayuda a un organismo a sobrevivir en su medio ambiente

**advantage** (ad van′ tij) a characteristic that can help an individual compete

**ventaja** característica que le permite a un individuo competir

## C

**characteristics** (kar′ ik tə ris′ tiks) the qualities an organism has

**rasgos** cualidades que tiene un organismo

**competition** (kom′ pə tish′ ən) occurs when two or more living things need the same resources in order to survive

**competencia** ocurre cuando dos o más seres vivos necesitan los mismos recursos para sobrevivir

**conduction** (kən duk′ shən) the transfer of heat that occurs when one thing touches another

**conducción** transmisión de calor que ocurre cuando un objeto toca otro objeto

**conductor** (kən duk′ tər) a material through which an electric charge can move easily

**conductor** material a través del cual las cargas eléctricas se mueven fácilmente

..................................................

**convection** (kən vek′ shən) the transfer of thermal energy as matter moves

**convección** transferencia de energía térmica mientras se mueve la materia

**design process** (di zīn′ pros′ es) a set of steps for developing products and processes that solve problems

**proceso de diseño** serie de pasos para desarrollar productos y procesos que resuelven problemas

..................................................

**drag** (drag) force that occurs when an object moves through a fluid

**resistencia aerodinámica** fuerza que ocurre cuando un objeto se mueve a través de un líquido

**E**

**electric current** (i lek′ trik  kėr′ ənt) an electric charge in motion

**corriente eléctrica** carga eléctrica en movimiento

..................................................

**energy** (en′ ər jē) the ability to cause motion or create change

**energía** capacidad de producir movimiento o causar cambio

..................................................

**environment** (en vī′ rən mənt) everything that surrounds a living thing

**medio ambiente** todo lo que rodea a un ser vivo

..................................................

**epicenter** (ep′ ə sen′ tər) point on Earth's surface that is directly above the focus of an earthquake

**epicentro** punto de la superficie de la Tierra directamente sobre el foco de un terremoto

..................................................

**erosion** (i rō′ zhən) process of carrying away weathered bits of rock

**erosión** proceso por el cual se mueven pedacitos de roca desgastada

**evidence** (ev′ ə dəns) observations and facts gained from experiments

**evidencia** observaciones y datos obtenidos de experimentos

**fault** (fȯlt) break or crack in rocks where Earth's crust can move suddenly

**falla** fisura o grieta en las rocas donde la corteza terrestre puede desplazarse en forma repentina

**filament** (fil′ ə mənt) a thin, coiled wire that can get very hot without melting

**filamento** alambre fino y enrollado que puede calentarse mucho sin derretirse

**focus** (fō′ kəs) place where plates start to slip

**foco** lugar donde las placas comienzan a deslizarse

**force** (fôrs) any push or pull

**fuerza** empujón o jalón

**friction** (frik′ shən) a force that acts when two surfaces rub together

**fricción** fuerza que actúa cuando dos superficies se rozan

**gravity** (grav′ ə tē) the force that pulls all objects toward each other

**gravedad** fuerza que atrae a todos los objetos entre sí

**humus** (hyü′ məs) a material in soil made up of decayed plants and animals

**humus** material que se encuentra en el suelo y está formado por plantas y animales descompuestos

**hypothesis** (hī poth′ ə sis) a possible answer to a question

**hipótesis** respuesta posible a una pregunta

**inference** (in′ fər əns) a conclusion drawn from data and observations

**inferencia** conclusión que se saca de los datos y de las observaciones

**inherit** (in her′ it) to receive characteristics from an organism's parents

**heredar** recibir rasgos de los padres de un organismo

**inquiry** (in kwī′ rē) the process of asking questions and searching for answers

**indagación** proceso que consiste en preguntar y buscar repuestas

**insulator** (in′ sə lā′ tər) a material through which an electric charge moves with difficulty

**aislante** material a través del cual las cargas eléctricas se mueven con dificultad

**investigation** (in ves′ tə gā′ shən) a careful way of looking for something

**investigación** manera cuidadosa de buscar algo

**kinetic energy (**kin net′ ik en′ ər jē) energy of motion

**energía cinética** energía de movimiento

**landform** (land′ fôrm) natural land feature on Earth's surface

**accidente geográfico** formación natural en la superficie terrestre

**lift** (lift) a pushing force from below that keeps an airplane in the air

**sustentación** fuerza que empuja desde abajo y que mantiene en el aire a los aviones

**M**

**motion** (mō′ shən) a change in the position of an object

**movimiento** cambio en la posición de un objeto

**N**

**nonnative** (non nā′ tiv) organisms that live outside of their usual habitats

**exótico** organismo que vive fuera de su hábitat natural

**nonrenewable resource** (non′ ri nü′ ə bəl rē′ sôrs) resource that exists in limited amounts or is used faster than it can be replaced in nature

**recurso no renovable** recurso que existe en cantidades limitadas o que se usa más rápido de lo que le toma a la naturaleza reponerlo

**P**

**parallel circuit** (par′ ə lel sėr′ kit) a circuit that has two or more paths through which electrical charges may flow

**circuito en paralelo** circuito que tiene dos o más vías por las que pueden fluir las cargas eléctricas

**pollution** (pə lü′ shən) waste from products made or used by people

**contaminación** desecho de los productos creados o usados por la gente

**potential energy** (pə ten′ shəl en′ ər jē) energy that is stored in an object

**energía potencial** energía que está almacenada en un objeto

**procedure** (prə sē′ jər) a set of step-by-step instructions

**procedimiento** instrucciones paso por paso

**prototype** (pro′ tə tīp) first fully working product that uses a design solution

**prototipo** el primer producto que demuestra una solución de diseño

## R

**radiation** (rā′ dē ā′ shən) energy that is sent out in waves

**radiación** energía transmitida a través de ondas

**reclamation** (rek′ lə mā′ shən) process of restoring land after it has been used

**recuperación** proceso en el cual se restaura la tierra después de que ha sido utilizada

**reference point** (ref′ ər əns point) a place or object used for determining if something is in motion

**punto de referencia** lugar u objeto usado para determinar si algo está en movimiento

**renewable resource** (ri nü′ ə bəl rē′ sôrs) resource that can be replaced

**recurso renovable** recurso que se puede reemplazar

## S

**scientific methods** (sī′ ən tif′ ik meth′ ədz) organized ways to answer questions and solve problems

**métodos científicos** maneras organizadas de responder a preguntas y resolver problemas

**series circuit** (sir′ ēz sér′ kit) a circuit in which electrical charge can only flow in one circular path

**circuito en serie** circuito en el cual las cargas eléctricas sólo pueden fluir en una trayectoria circular

**speed** (spēd) the rate at which an object changes position

**rapidez** ritmo al cual cambia la posición de un objeto

**stimulus** (stim′ yə ləs) something that causes a reaction in a living thing

**estímulo** algo que provoca una reacción en un ser vivo

**technology** (tek nol′ ə jē) the knowledge, processes, and products that solve problems and make work easier

**tecnología** el conocimiento, los procesos y los productos con que se resuelven los problemas y se facilita el trabajo

**three-dimensional** (thrē′ də men′ shə nəl) describes objects that have length, width, and height

**tridimensional** describe objetos que tienen largo, ancho y altura

**thrust** (thrust) force that pushes or pulls an airplane forward

**empuje** fuerza que empuja o jala un avión hacia delante

**tool** (tül) an object or device used to perform a task.

**instrumento** objeto o herramienta que se usa para hacer un trabajo

**two-dimensional** (tü′ də men′ shə nəl) describes something that has length and width, but not height

**bidimensional** describe algo que tiene largo y ancho, pero no tiene altura

**velocity** (və los′ ə tē) the speed and the direction an object is moving

**velocidad** rapidez y dirección en que se mueve un objeto

**volcano** (vol kā′ nō) opening in Earth's crust where gases, ash, and molten rock can reach the surface

**volcán** abertura de la corteza terrestre por el cual gases, cenizas y rocas fundidas pueden alcanzar la superficie

**weathering** (we‭н′ ər ing) process of rocks in Earth's crust slowly being broken into smaller pieces

**meteorización** proceso de las rocas de la corteza terrestre que se van rompiendo en trozos más pequeños

# Index

This index lists the pages on which a topic appears. Page numbers following a *p* refer to a photograph or illustration. Page numbers following a *c* refer to a chart or graph.

# Credits

## Staff Credits

The people who made up the *Interactive Science* team — representing composition services, core design digital and multimedia production services, digital product development, editorial, editorial services, manufacturing, and production — are listed below.

Geri Amani, Alisa Anderson, Jose Arrendondo, Amy Austin, Scott Baker, Lindsay Bellino, Charlie Bink, Bridget Binstock, Holly Blessen, Robin Bobo, Craig Bottomley, Jim Brady, Laura Brancky, Chris Budzisz, Mary Chingwa, Sitha Chhor, Caroline Chung, Margaret Clampitt, Kier Cline, Brandon Cole, Mitch Coulter, AnnMarie Coyne, Fran Curran, Dana Damiano, Nancy Duffner, Amanda Ferguson, David Gall, Mark Geyer, Amy Goodwin, Gerardine Griffin, Chris Haggerty, Laura Hancko, Jericho Hernandez, Autumn Hickenlooper, Guy Huff, George Jacobson, Marian Jones, Kathi Kalina, Chris Kammer, Sheila Kanitsch, Alyse Kondrat, Mary Kramer, Thea Limpus, Dominique Mariano, Lori McGuire, Melinda Medina, Angelina Mendez, Claudi Mimo, John Moore, Phoebe Novak, Anthony Nuccio, Jeffrey Osier, Julianne Regnier, Charlene Rimsa, Rebecca Roberts, Camille Salerno, Manuel Sanchez, Carol Schmitz, Amanda Seldera, Sheetal Shah, Jeannine Shelton El, Geri Shulman, Greg Sorenson, Samantha Sparkman, Mindy Spelius, Karen Stockwell, Dee Sunday, Dennis Tarwood, Jennie Teece, Lois Teesdale, Michaela Tudela, Oscar Vera, Dave Wade, Tom Wickland, James Yagelski, Tim Yetzina, Diane Zimmermann

## Illustrations

89, 164, 165 Peter Bollinger; 181, 215 Sharon & Joel Harris; 182, 185, 218, 239 Adam Benton; 198, 240 Precision Graphics; 232 Robert Ulrich

All other illustrations Chandler Digital Art

## Photographs

Every effort has been made to secure permission and provide appropriate credit for photographic material. The publisher deeply regrets any omission and pledges to correct errors called to its attention in subsequent editions.

Unless otherwise acknowledged, all photographs are the property of Pearson Education, Inc.

Photo locators denoted as follows: Top (T), Center (C), Bottom (B), Left (L), Right (R), Background (Bkgd)

**COVER:** ©Woodystock/Alamy

2 ©Kris Butler/Shutterstock, (C) ©Morgan Lane Photography/Shutterstock; 6 (TR) ©Inga Spence/Alamy Images, (BL) Demetrio Carrasco/©DK Images; 9 (CR) ©Harald Sund/Getty Images; 16 (TR) ©Grant Faint/Getty Images; 17 (BR) ©Maria Stenzel/National Geographic Image Collection; 24 (TR) ©Alexis Rosenfeld/Photo Researchers, Inc.; 25 (BR) ©Photoroller/ Shutterstock; 28 (BC) ©Alyda De Villers/iStockphoto, (BR) ©DK Images, (TR) ©Leslie Banks/iStockphoto, (BCL) Jupiter Images, (BL) Tim Ridley/©DK Images; 30 ©image100/Alamy; 34 (Bkgd) ©Don Farrall/Getty Images, (B) The African American Registry®; 35 (CR) ©Harald Sund/Getty Images, (TL) ©Maria Stenzel/National Geographic Image Collection, (CR) ©Robbie Shone/Alamy Images; 39 (Bkgd) ©Morgan Lane Photography/Shutterstock; 43 (Bkgd) ©Alexey Stiop/Shutterstock, (C) ©Image Source; 44 ©Jason South/Fairfaxphotos/The New York Times /Redux Pictures; 47 ©Andrew Holt/Getty Images, ©Gary Crabbe/Alamy Images; 48 (BL) ©Dieter Wanke/Alamy Images, (T) ©Neo Edmund/Shutterstock, (BCL) ©Steve Allen/Jupiter Images, (CL) URC Media; 49 (CR) ©Anthony Berenyi/Shutterstock; 52 ©Thomas Northcut/Thinkstock, Jupiterimages/Thinkstock; 53 Khromov Alexey/Shutterstock, Nicola Armstrong/Alamy; 54 Stefan Wackerhagen/Alamy Images; 55 Bayne Stanley/Alamy Images; 56 Library of Congress; 57 Goolia Photography/Alamy, Library of Congress, Tomas Kopecny/Alamy Images, Weberfoto/Alamy Images; 58 Israelimages/Alamy Images, LaRC/NASA; 59 Library of Congress; 60 Library of Congress; 61 Peter Bowater/Alamy Images; 64 ©Peter Casolino/Alamy Images, Ron Felt, Georgia Tech/©AP Images; 65 (TR) ©Anthony Berenyi/Shutterstock, (BR) LaRC/NASA; 67 ©Jason South/Fairfaxphotos/The New York Times /Redux Pictures; 71 ©Masterfile Royalty-Free; 76 (T) ©Ted Kinsman/Photo Researchers, Inc.; 77 (CR) Getty Images; 78 ©eldirector77/Shutterstock; 80 ©Peter Cade/Getty Images; 81 (TR) ©Imagemore Co., Ltd./Alamy; 88 (T) China Images/Alamy Images; 90 (B, ) Jane Burton/DK Images; 91 (TR) ©StonePhotos/Shutterstock; 92 (TR) ©Bryan Eastham/Shutterstock, (B) Getty Images; 93 (B) ©Jane Rix/Shutterstock; 94 (B) ©Marvin Dembinsky Photo Associates/Alamy; 99 (TL) ©VisionsofAmerica/Joe Sohm/Getty Images; 110 ©Glow Images/SuperStock; 112 ©Mark Scott/Getty Images; 114 (TL) ©Iconotec/Alamy; 128 (B) Getty Images; 129 (T) ©VisionsofAmerica/Joe Sohm/Getty Images; 135 (CL) ©DK Images; 136 (T) ©Alistair Scott/Alamy Images; 137 (TR) MSFC/NASA; 138 (R) ©AMA/Shutterstock, (CR) Jupiter Images; 141 (R) ©Alistair Scott/Alamy Images, (TL) ©Marvin Dembinsky Photo Associates/Alamy; 143 (B) ©Mark Scott/Getty Images; 147 (C) Photolibrary Group, Inc.; 148 ©Raul Touzon/Getty Images; 151 ©Laurentiu Iordache/Alamy; 152 (T) ©Pete Ryan/Getty Images; 153 (CR) ©Cade Martin/Getty Images; 154 (TL) ©TebNad/Shutterstock, (BL) ©U.P.images_photo/Shutterstock, (C) Jupiter Images; 155 (TR) ©Michael Stokes/Shutterstock, (CR) ©Trutta/Shutterstock; 160 (B) Jupiter Images; 161 (CR) ©National Geographic Image Collection/Alamy; 162 (B) ©Glenda M. Powers/Shutterstock; 163 (BR) ©D. Hurst/Alamy, (TR) ©john rensten/Alamy, (CL) ©Peter Cavanagh / Alamy/Alamy Images; 164 (T) DK Images; 166 (T) ©chris brignell / Alamy/Alamy Images, (T) ©geogphotos/Alamy; 167 (CR) ©blackpixel/Shutterstock, (BR) James Stevenson/©DK Images; 168 (TL) ©Cameron/Corbis, ©Savanah Stewart/Danita Delimont/Alamy; 169 ©Big Cheese Photo LLC/Alamy; 170 ©kavram/Shutterstock; 172 (T) ©Kinsman Physics Productions, (CL) ©Ted Soqui/Corbis, (B) Photograph courtesy of Dr. Nick Hudyma (University of North Florida and Dr. Dennis Hiltunen (University of Florida); 173 (BL) ©Michael S. Quinton/Getty Images, Liam Gumley, Space Science Engineering Center, University of Wisconsin - Madison

This is your book.

You can write in it.

# Take Note

This space is yours. It is great for drawing diagrams and making notes.